play guitar with...

AF378618

the dandy warhols, muse, pulp, ash, travis and feeder

bohemian like you 4
the dandy warhols

12 **burn baby burn** ash

feeder **just a day** 24

18 **plug in baby** muse

33 **side** travis

pulp **sunrise** 40

Wise Publications
London/New York/Paris/Sydney/Copenhagen/Berlin/Madrid/Tokyo

guitar tablature explained

Guitar music can be notated three different ways: on a musical stave, in tablature, and in rhythm slashes

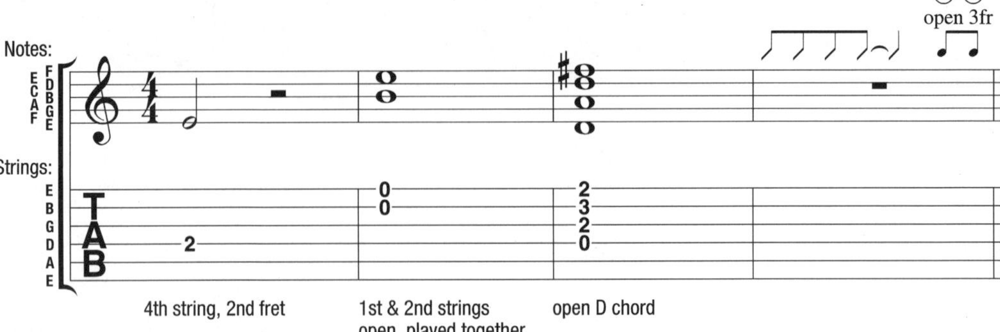

RHYTHM SLASHES are written above the stave. Strum chords in the rhythm indicated. Round noteheads indicate single notes.

THE MUSICAL STAVE shows pitches and rhythms and is divided by lines into bars. Pitches are named after the first seven letters of the alphabet.

TABLATURE graphically represents the guitar fingerboard. Each horizontal line represents a string, and each number represents a fret.

definitions for special guitar notation

SEMI-TONE BEND: Strike the note and bend up a semi-tone (1/2 step).

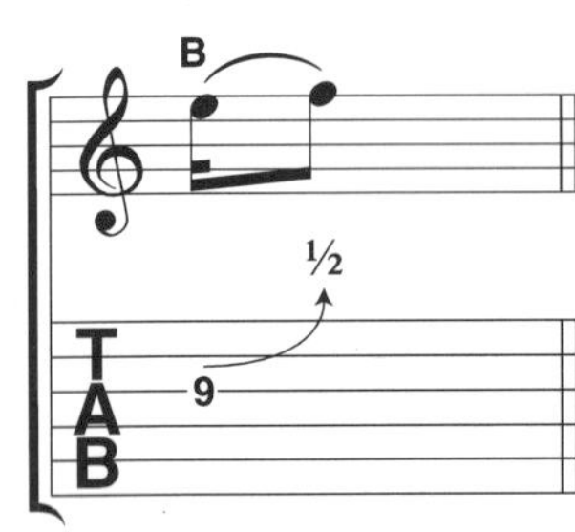

WHOLE-TONE BEND: Strike the note and bend up a whole-tone (whole step).

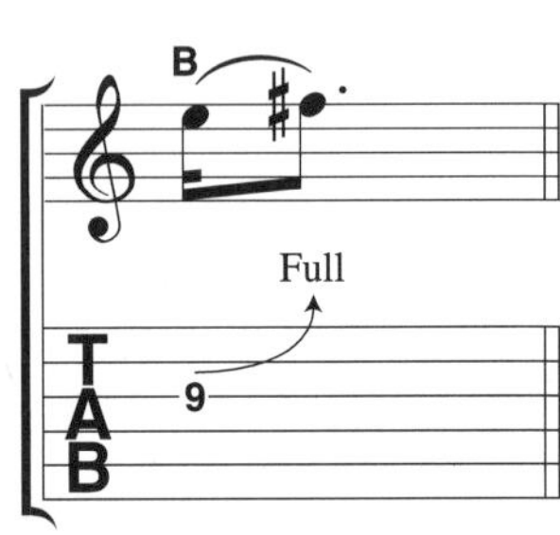

GRACE NOTE BEND: Strike the note and bend as indicated. Play the first note as quickly as possible.

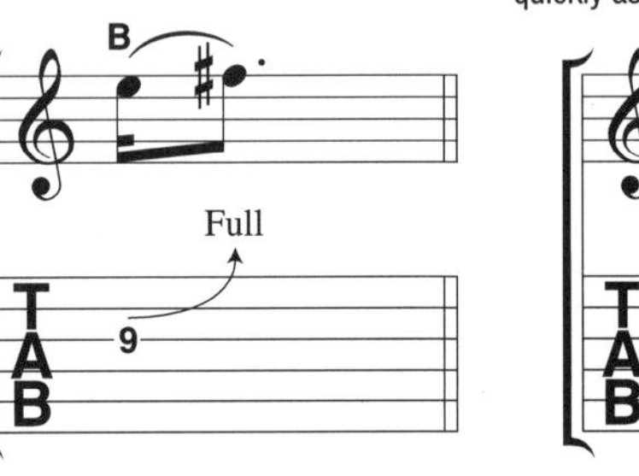

QUARTER-TONE BEND: Strike the note and bend up a 1/4 step.

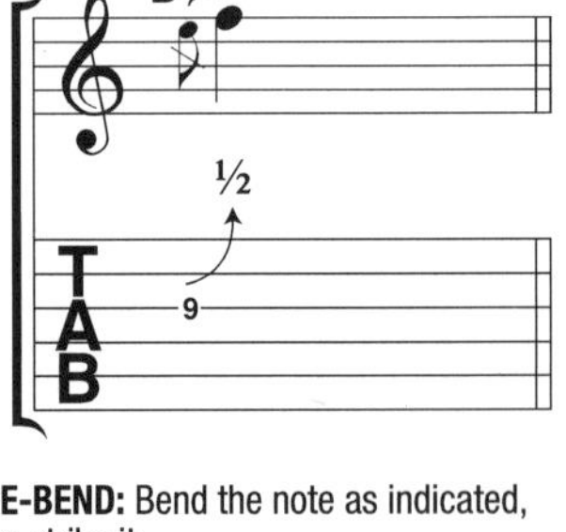

BEND & RELEASE: Strike the note and bend up as indicated, then release back to the original note.

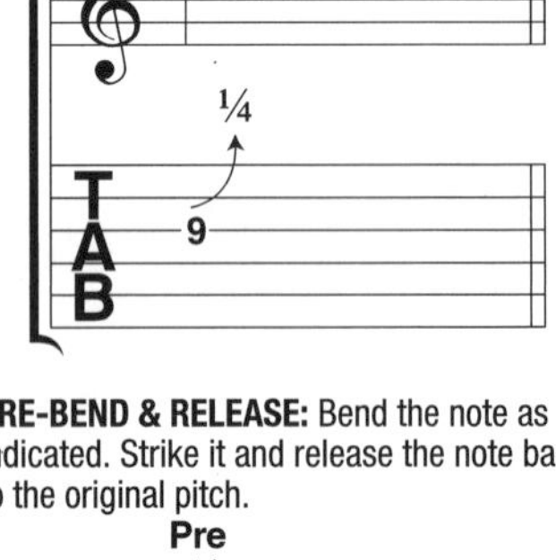

COMPOUND BEND & RELEASE: Strike the note and bend up and down in the rhythm indicated.

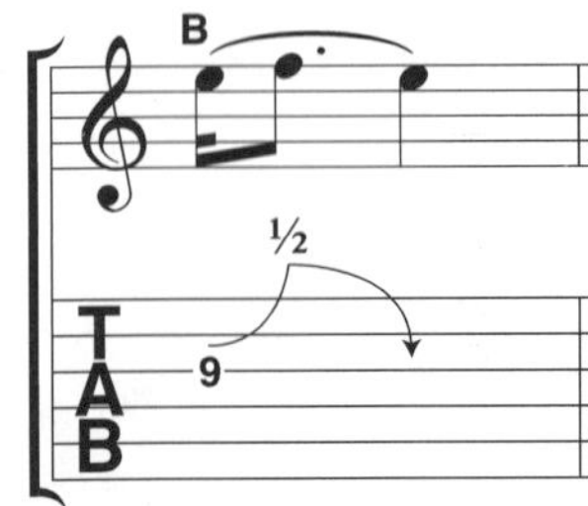

PRE-BEND: Bend the note as indicated, then strike it.

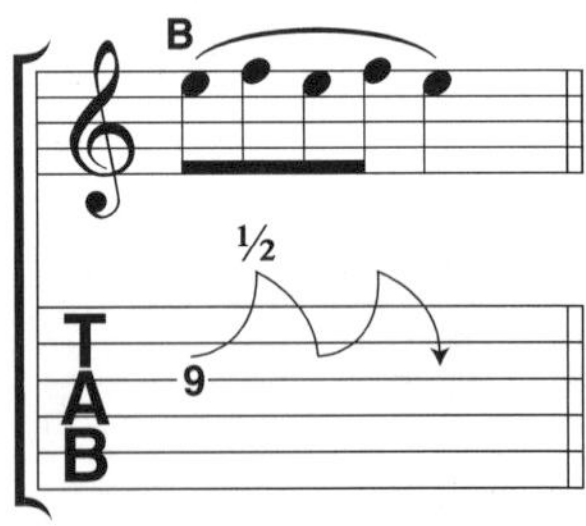

PRE-BEND & RELEASE: Bend the note as indicated. Strike it and release the note back to the original pitch.

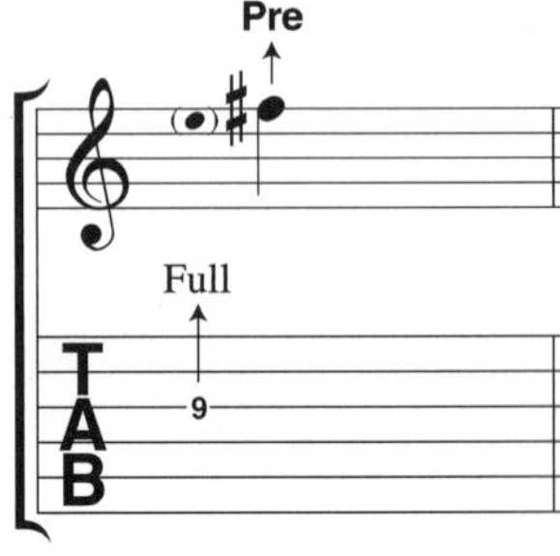

UNISON BEND: Strike the two notes simultaneously and bend the lower note up to the pitch of the higher.

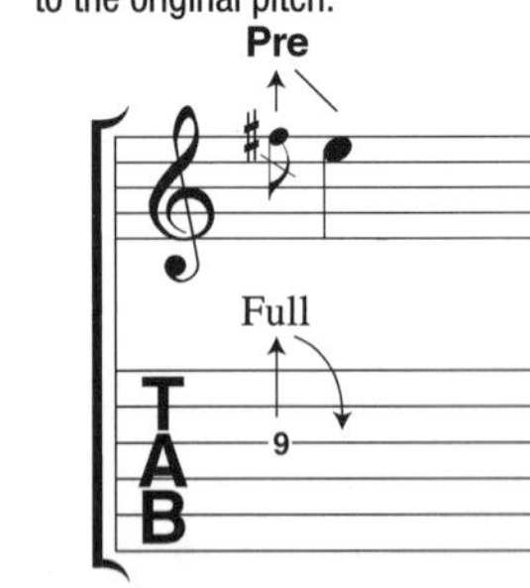

BEND & RESTRIKE: Strike the note and bend as indicated then restrike the string where the symbol occurs.

BEND, HOLD AND RELEASE: Same as bend and release but hold the bend for the duration of the tie.

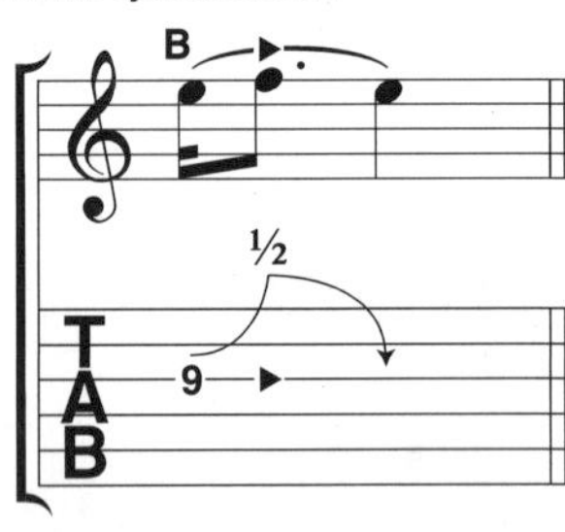

BEND AND TAP: Bend the note as indicated and tap the higher fret while still holding the bend.

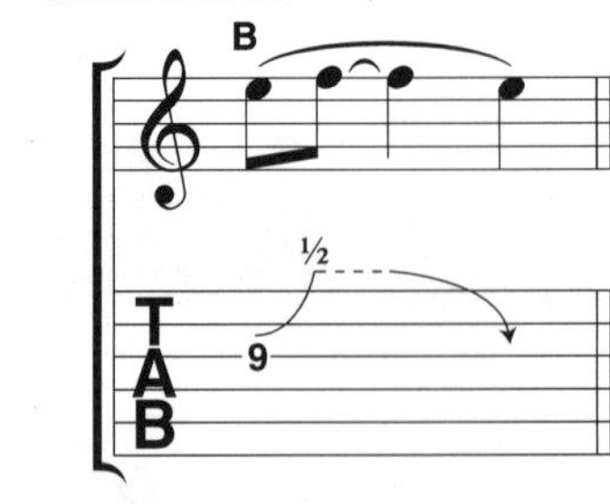

VIBRATO: The string is vibrated by rapidly bending and releasing the note with the fretting hand.

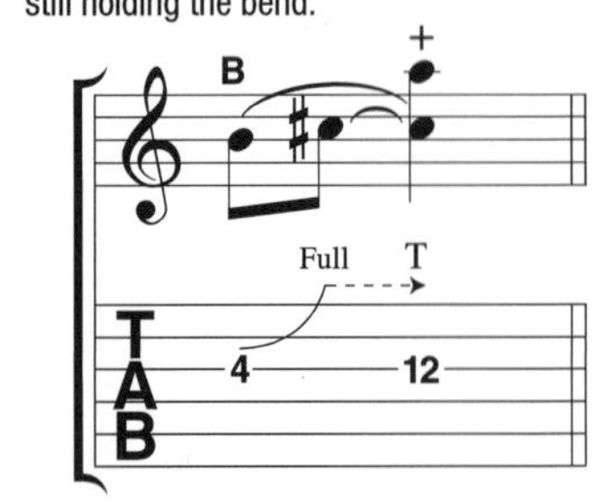

HAMMER-ON: Strike the first (lower) note with one finger, then sound the higher note (on the same string) with another finger by fretting it without picking.

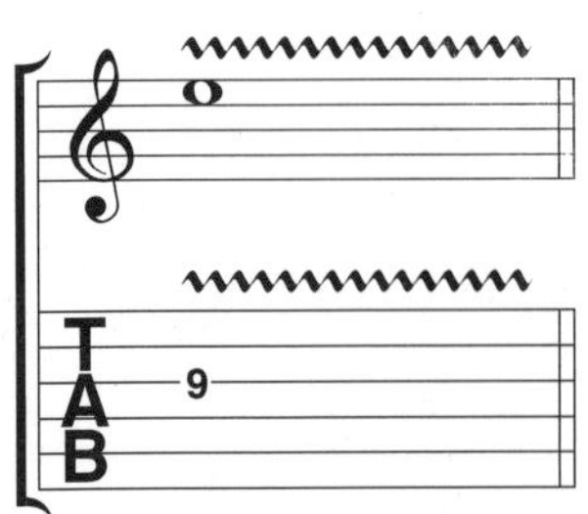

PULL-OFF: Place both fingers on the notes to be sounded, Strike the first note and without picking, pull the finger off to sound the second (lower) note.

LEGATO SLIDE (GLISS): Strike the first note and then slide the same fret-hand finger up or down to the second note. The second note is not struck.

NOTE: The speed of any bend is indicated by the music notation and tempo.

SHIFT SLIDE (GLISS & RESTRIKE): Same as legato slide, except the second note is struck.

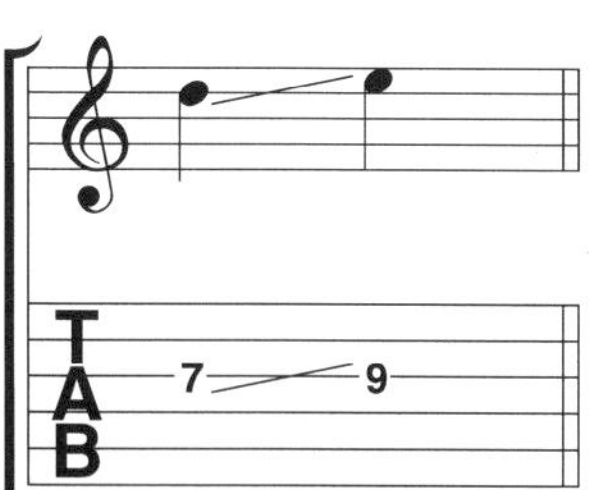

TRILL: Very rapidly alternate between the notes indicated by continuously hammering on and pulling off.

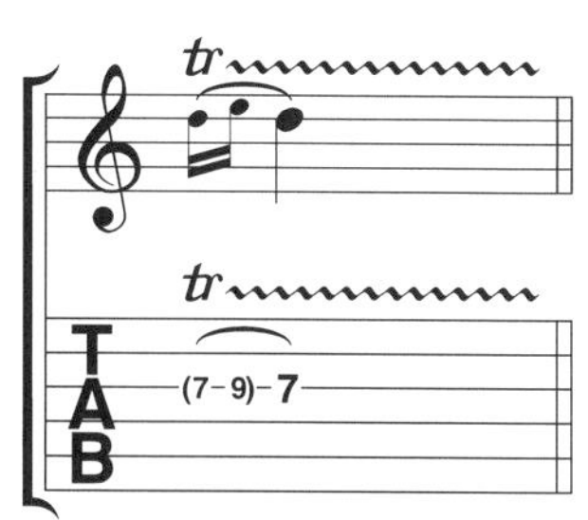

TAPPING: Hammer ("tap") the fret indicated with the pick-hand index or middle finger and pull off to the note fretted by the fret hand.

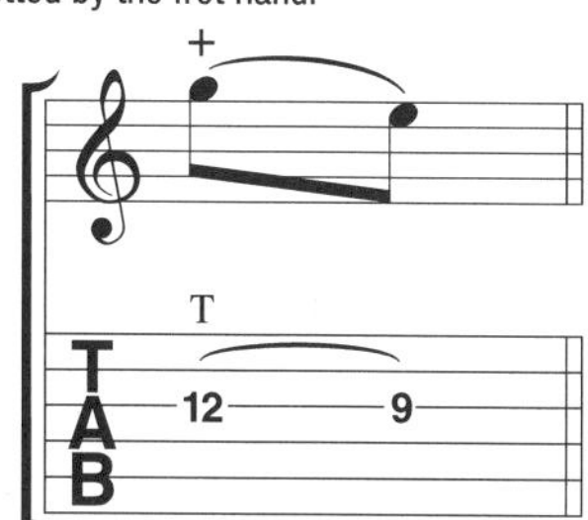

PICK SCRAPE: The edge of the pick is rubbed down (or up) the string, producing a scratchy sound.

MUFFLED STRINGS: A percussive sound is produced by laying the fret hand across the string(s) without depressing, and striking them with the pick hand.

NATURAL HARMONIC: Strike the note while the fret-hand lightly touches the string directly over the fret indicated.

PINCH HARMONIC: The note is fretted normally and a harmonic is produced by adding the edge of the thumb or the tip of the index finger of the pick hand to the normal pick attack.

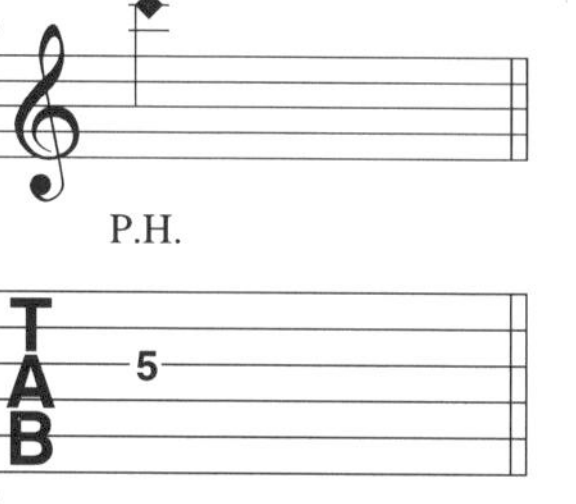

HARP HARMONIC: The note is fretted normally and a harmonic is produced by gently resting the pick hand's index finger directly above the indicated fret (in parentheses) while the pick hand's thumb or pick assists by plucking the appropriate string.

PALM MUTING: The note is partially muted by the pick hand lightly touching the string(s) just before the bridge.

RAKE: Drag the pick across the strings indicated with a single motion.

TREMOLO PICKING: The note is picked as rapidly and continuously as possible.

ARPEGGIATE: Play the notes of the chord indicated by quickly rolling them from bottom to top.

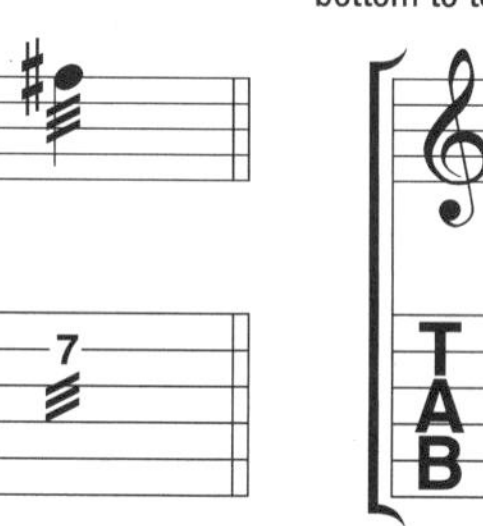

SWEEP PICKING: Rhythmic downstroke and/or upstroke motion across the strings.

VIBRATO DIVE BAR AND RETURN: The pitch of the note or chord is dropped a specific number of steps (in rhythm) then returned to the original pitch.

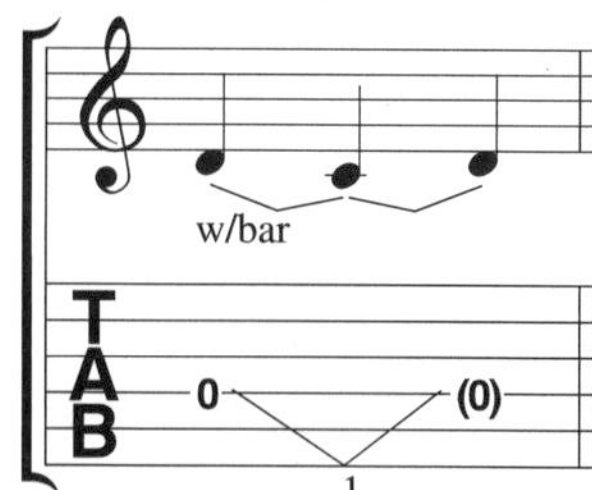

VIBRATO BAR SCOOP: Depress the bar just before striking the note, then quickly release the bar.

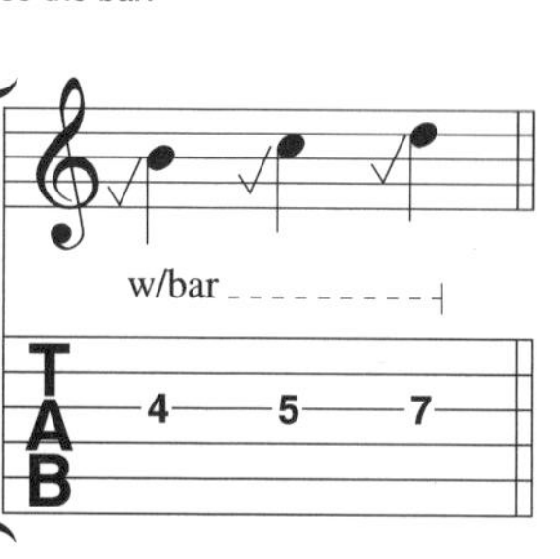

VIBRATO BAR DIP: Strike the note and then immediately drop a specific number of steps, then release back to the original pitch.

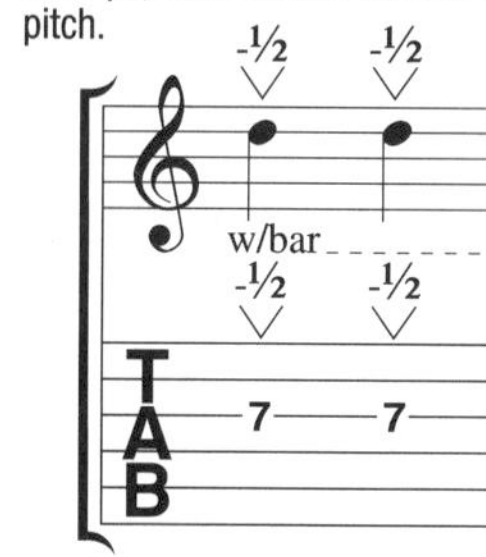

additional musical definitions

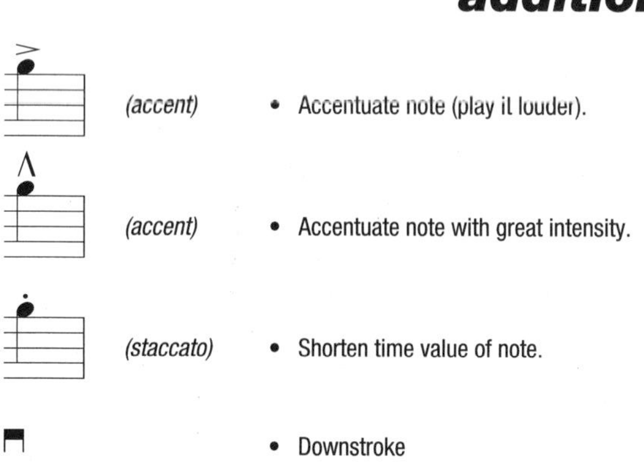

(accent) • Accentuate note (play it louder).

(accent) • Accentuate note with great intensity.

(staccato) • Shorten time value of note.

• Downstroke

V • Upstroke

D.%. al Coda

• Go back to the sign (%), then play until the bar marked *To Coda* ⊕ then skip to the section marked ⊕ *Coda*.

D.C. al Fine

• Go back to the beginning of the song and play until the bar marked *Fine* (end).

tacet

• Instrument is silent (drops out).

• Repeat bars between signs.

1. **2.**

• When a repeated section has different endings, play the first ending only the first time and the second ending only the second time.

NOTE: Tablature numbers in parentheses mean:
1. The note is sustained, but a new articulation (such as hammer on or slide) begins.
2. A note may be fretted but not necessarily played.

bohemian like you

Words & Music by Courtney Taylor-Taylor

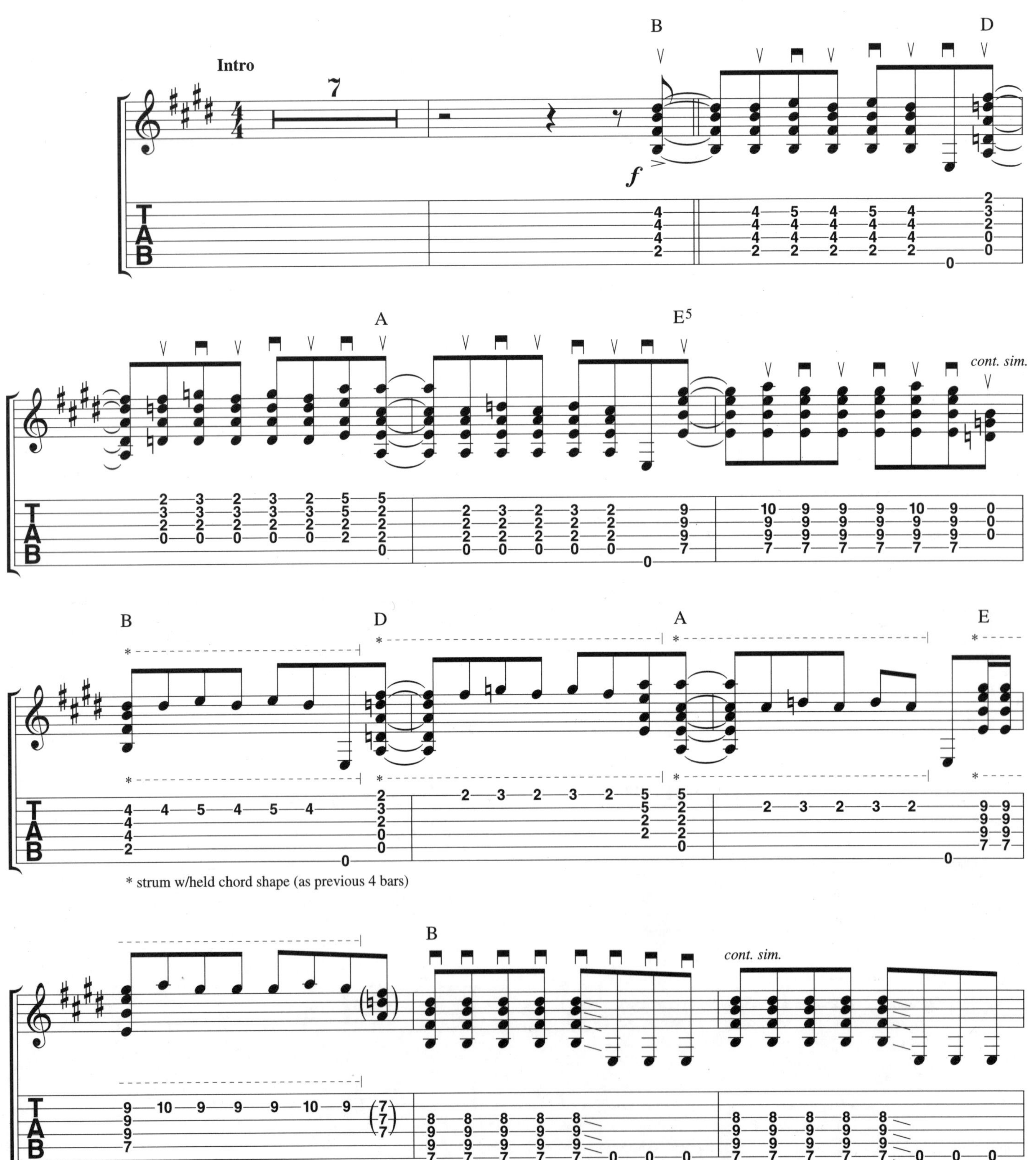

B
D5
1. You've got a great car, yeah, what's
Oh, yeah
mf w/slight P.M.
A
E5
wrong with it to-day, I used to have one too, may-be I'll
I wait ta-bles too, no I have-n't heard your band, 'cause you
B
D5
come and have a look. I real-ly love your hair
guys are pret-ty new. But if you dig, on
A
E5
do yeah, I'm glad you like mine too, see we're
ve-gan food well come ov-er to my work I'll have them

1.
B5
look - in' pret - ty cool, get ya?
cook you some - thing that you real - ly
f
1. cont.
2. So what do you do?
2. Chorus   B   D5   A   E5
love   'cause I like___ you,   yeah I like___ you,   and I'm feel -
B   D5   A
- in' so bo - he - mi - an like___ you,   yeah I like___ you,   yeah I like___

you, and I feel whoa-ho. Woo!
* strum w/held chord shape as previously
Ooh oo ooh.
Ooh ooh ooh.
Ooh ooh ooh.
Ooh ooh ooh.
cont. sim.

Verse
(B5)
(Wait) 3. Who's that guy just
mp optional . . . .
(D5)   (A5)   (E5)
hang-in' at your pad? He's look-in' kind-a bummed, yeah you broke up, that's too bad. I guess it's
(B5)   (D5)   (A5)
fair   if he al-ways pays the rent   and he does-n't get bent a-'bout
Chorus
(E5)   B5   D5   A5
sleep-in' on the couch when I'm there.   'Cause I like____ you,   yeah I like__
f

you, and I'm feel - in' so bo - he - mi - an like you, yeah I like
you, yeah I like you, and I feel whoa-ho. Woo!
Ooh oo ooh.
* strum w/held chord shape as previously
Ooh ooh ooh.
Ooh ooh ooh.

E   B
I'm get - tin' wise and I
And I like

D   A
feel so bo - he - mi - an like you,   it's you   and I like
you   and I like   you,   and I like

E   B
that I want   so   please   just a cas -
you, I like you,   you I like   you I like   you I like

1.

D   A   E
u - al, cas - u - al ea - sy thing.   Is   it? It is   for me
you I like you, I like you   and I feel

Outro
E   B   D   A
whoa-ho.   Woo!   Ooh oo   ooh.
8va
* strum w/held chord shape as previously
E   B   D
Ooh ooh   ooh.
A   E   B
Ooh ooh   ooh.   Ooh ooh   ooh.

burn baby burn

Words & Music by Tim Wheeler

© Copyright 2001 Universal/Island Music Limited, Elsinore House, 77 Fulham Palace Road, London W6 8JA.
All Rights Reserved. International Copyright Secured.

Verse
B5   E5   C#5   F#5   B5   E5

have   in this teen-age twi-light,_____   your gold-en hair and your pale blue eyes,_____
2. walk   like you're in a daze,_____   un-res-pon-sive eyes   in a dis - tant gaze,_____

mf w/P.M.
* optional, doubling Gtr.2

C#5   F#5   B5   E5   C#5   F#5

but through all the days   and the sleep - less nights,_____   we have
like   all   the good   times have flown a - way,_____   and memo -

Em   F#5   B   E

nev - er been sa - tis - fied._____   Tum - bl-ing like the leaves_
-ry leaves a bit - ter taste._____   Tum - bl-ing like the leaves_

f

C#   F#   B   E   C#   F#

yeah we are spir - al - ing on the breeze,_____   al - most to the
yeah we are spir - al - ing on the breeze,_____   des - truc - tive

B
E
C#
F#
Em
point of no re - turn, ev - 'ry-thing will burn ba - by burn.
love is all we have, des - truc - tive love is all I am.
Chorus
F#m
B
Look in - to my tired eyes, see some -
E
A
G#m
F#m
- one you don't re - cog - nise. Binds that can't be un - tied,
B
E
A
G#m
oh this is slow su - i - cide. Feel -

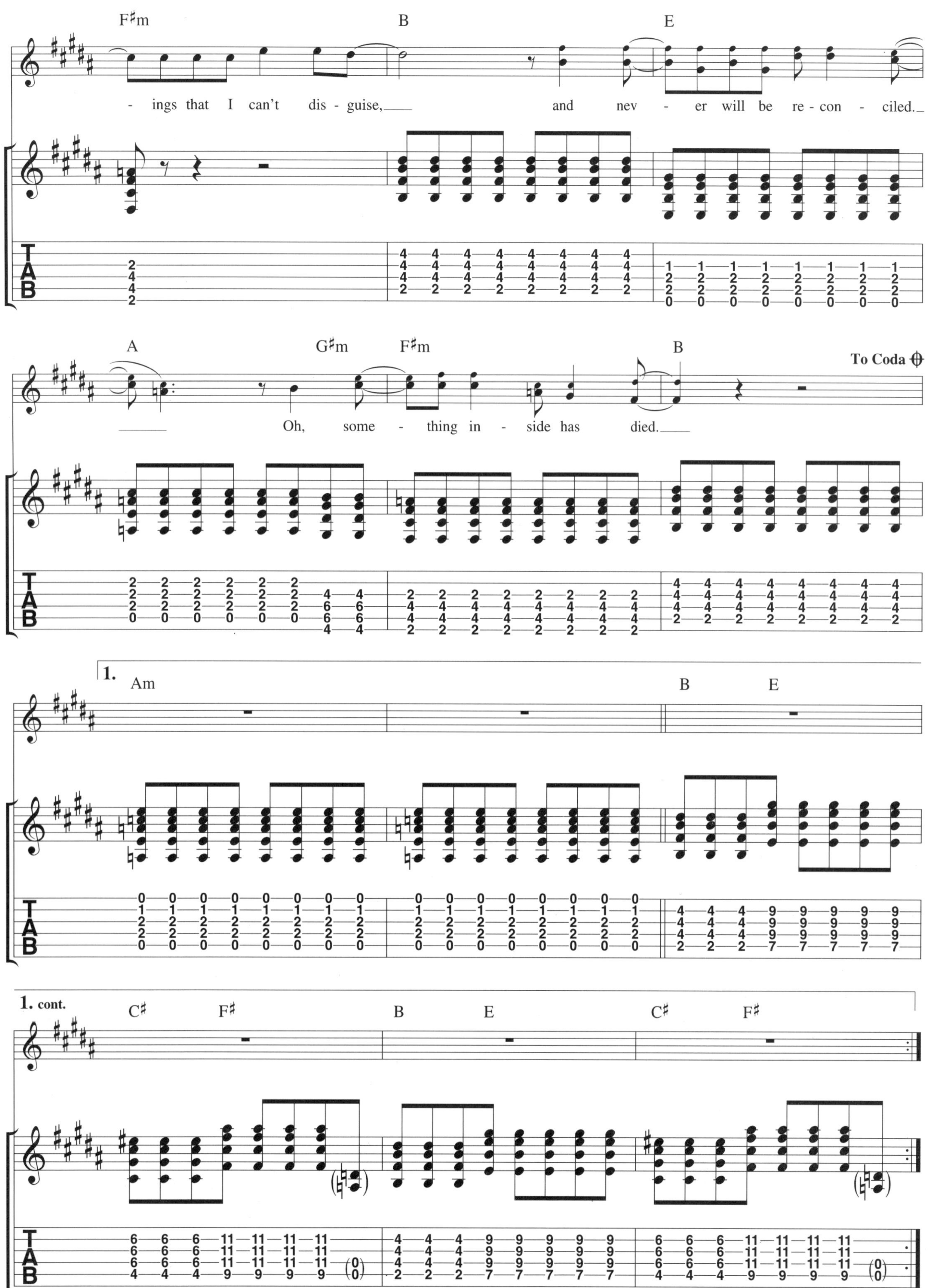

F#m   B   E
- ings that I can't dis - guise,   and nev - er will be re - con - ciled.

A   G#m   F#m   B   To Coda
Oh, some - thing in - side has died.

1.
Am   B   E

1. cont.
C#   F#   B   E   C#   F#

2.
Solo
Am
B E
C# F#
B E
C# F#
B E
C# F#
B E
C# F#
8va
gradual bend
½
½
½
Bridge
E5
F#5
E5
Vi - cious bit - ter words be - com - ing more and more cruel,
mf w/P.M.
F#5
E5
F#5
but you al - ways take it back, you

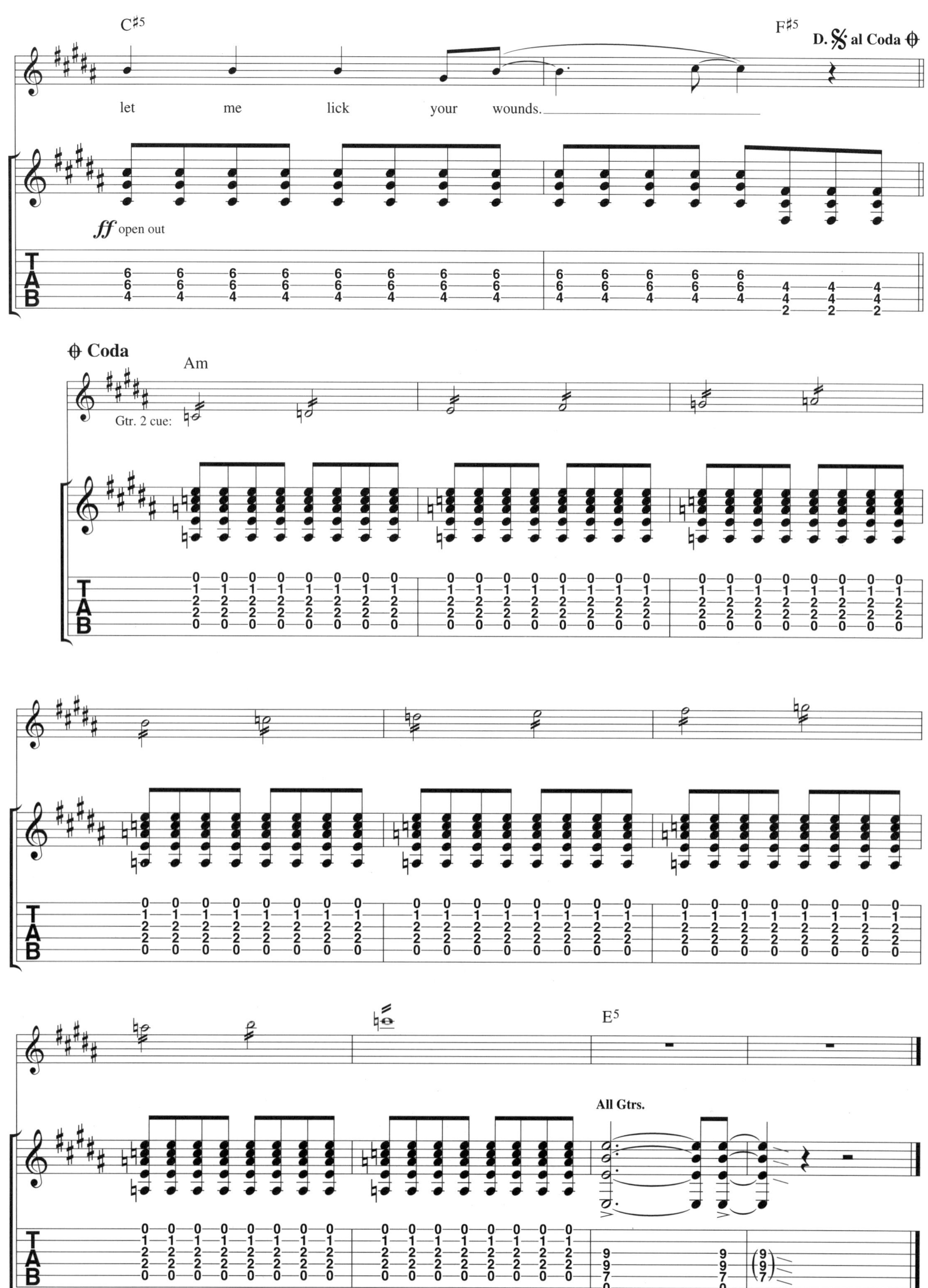

C#5
F#5
D. S al Coda
let me lick your wounds.
ff open out
Coda
Am
Gtr. 2 cue:
All Gtrs.
E5

plug in baby

Lyrics & Music by Matthew Bellamy

Intro

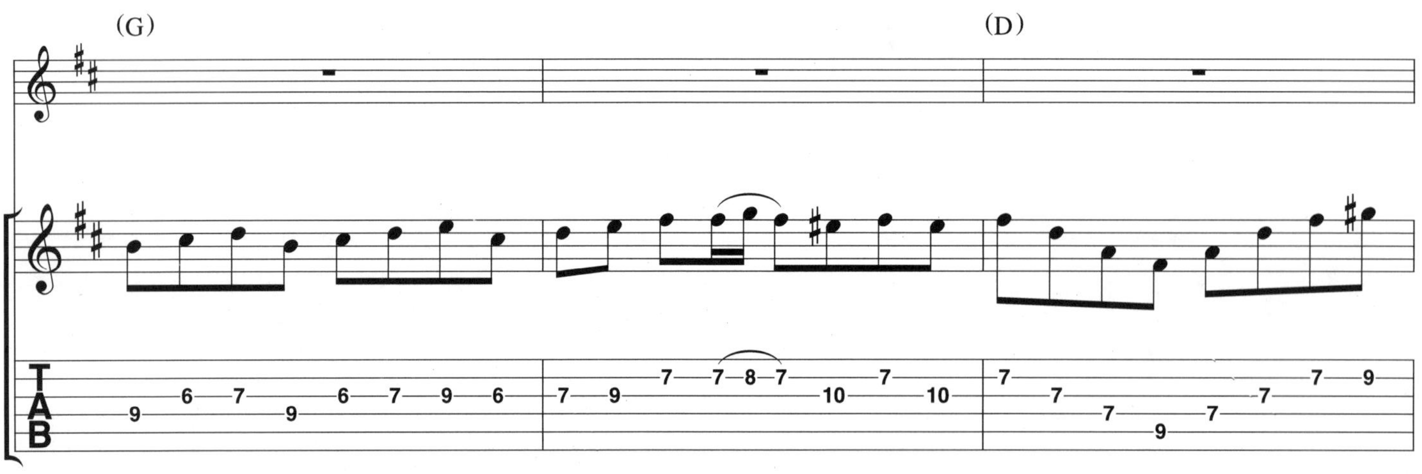

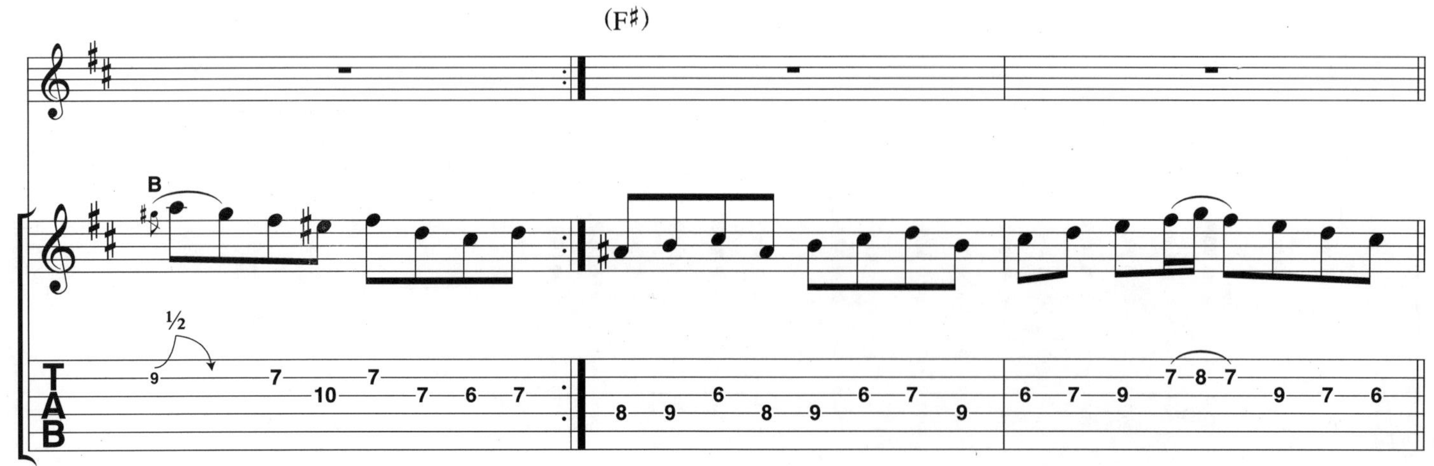

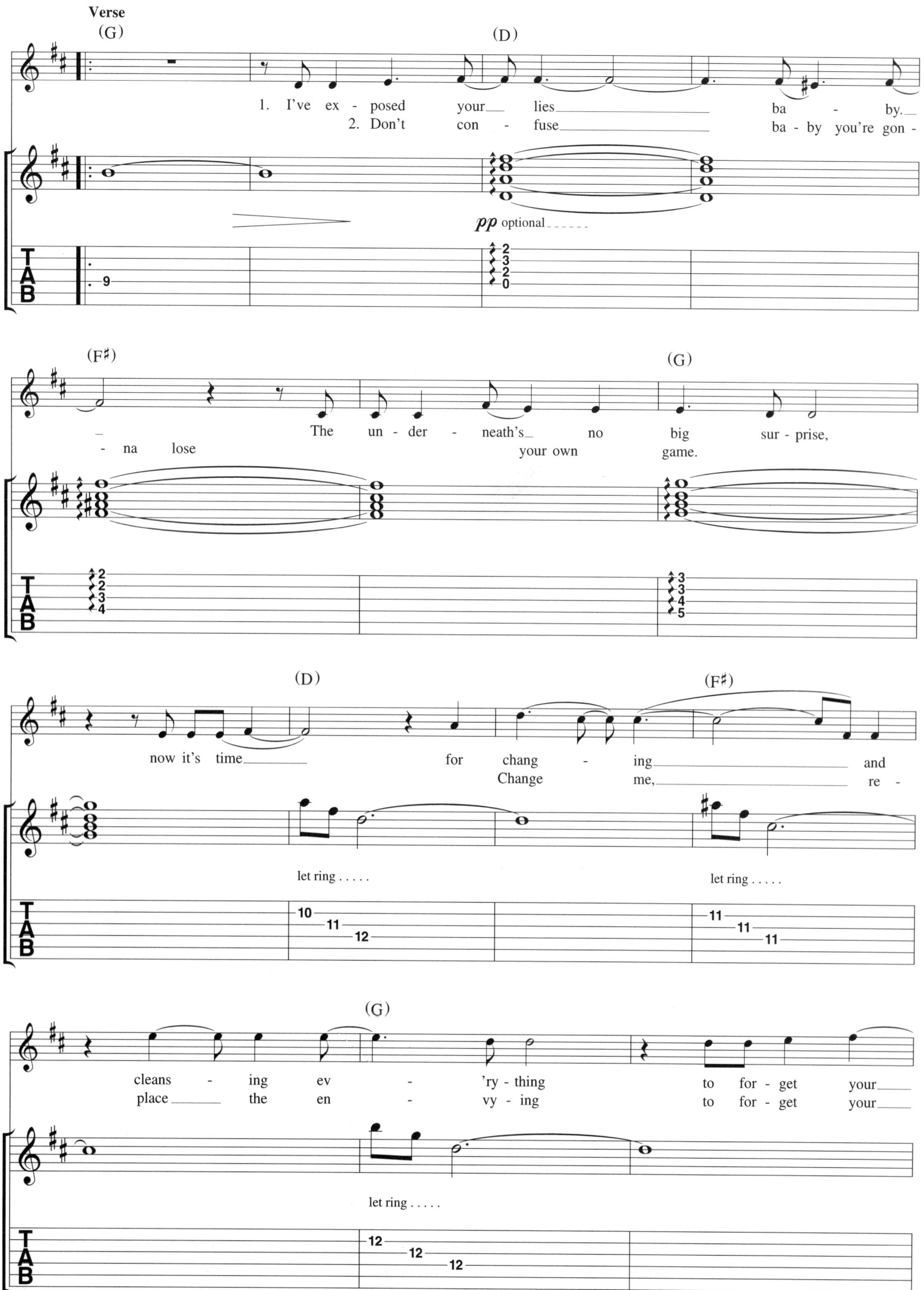

Verse
(G)
(D)
1. I've ex - posed your lies ba - by.
2. Don't con - fuse ba - by you're gon -
pp optional
9
(F#)
(G)
- na lose
The un - der - neath's no big sur - prise,
your own game.
(D)
(F#)
now it's time for chang - ing and
Change me, re -
let ring . . . . .
let ring . . . . .
10
11
12
11
11
11
(G)
cleans - ing ev - 'ry - thing to for - get your
place the en - vy - ing to for - get your
let ring . . . . .
12
12
12

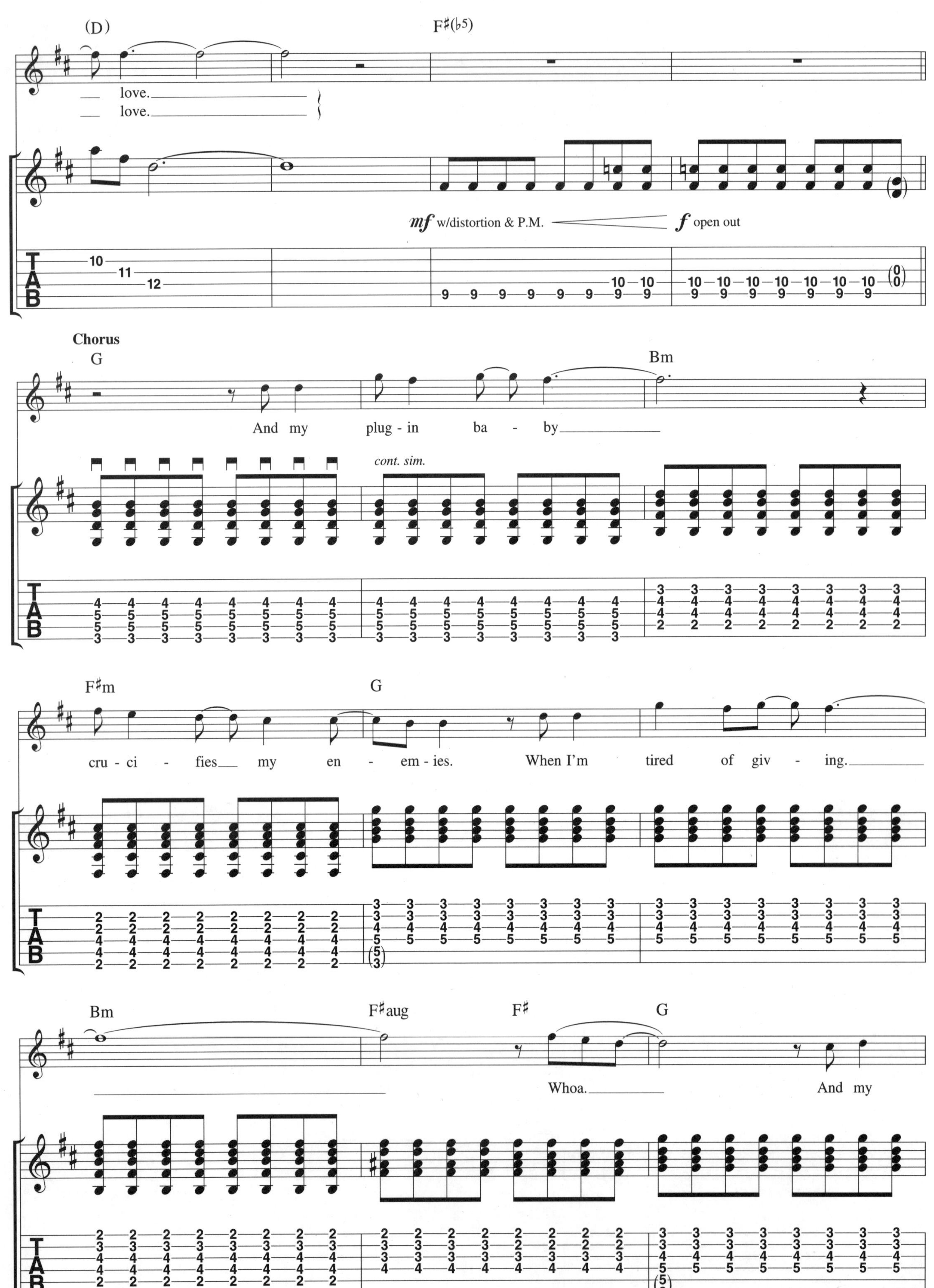
(D)
F#(b5)
love.
love.
mf w/distortion & P.M.
f open out
Chorus
G
Bm
And my plug-in ba - by
cont. sim.
F#m
G
cru - ci - fies my en - em - ies. When I'm tired of giv - ing.
Bm
F#aug
F#
G
Whoa.
And my

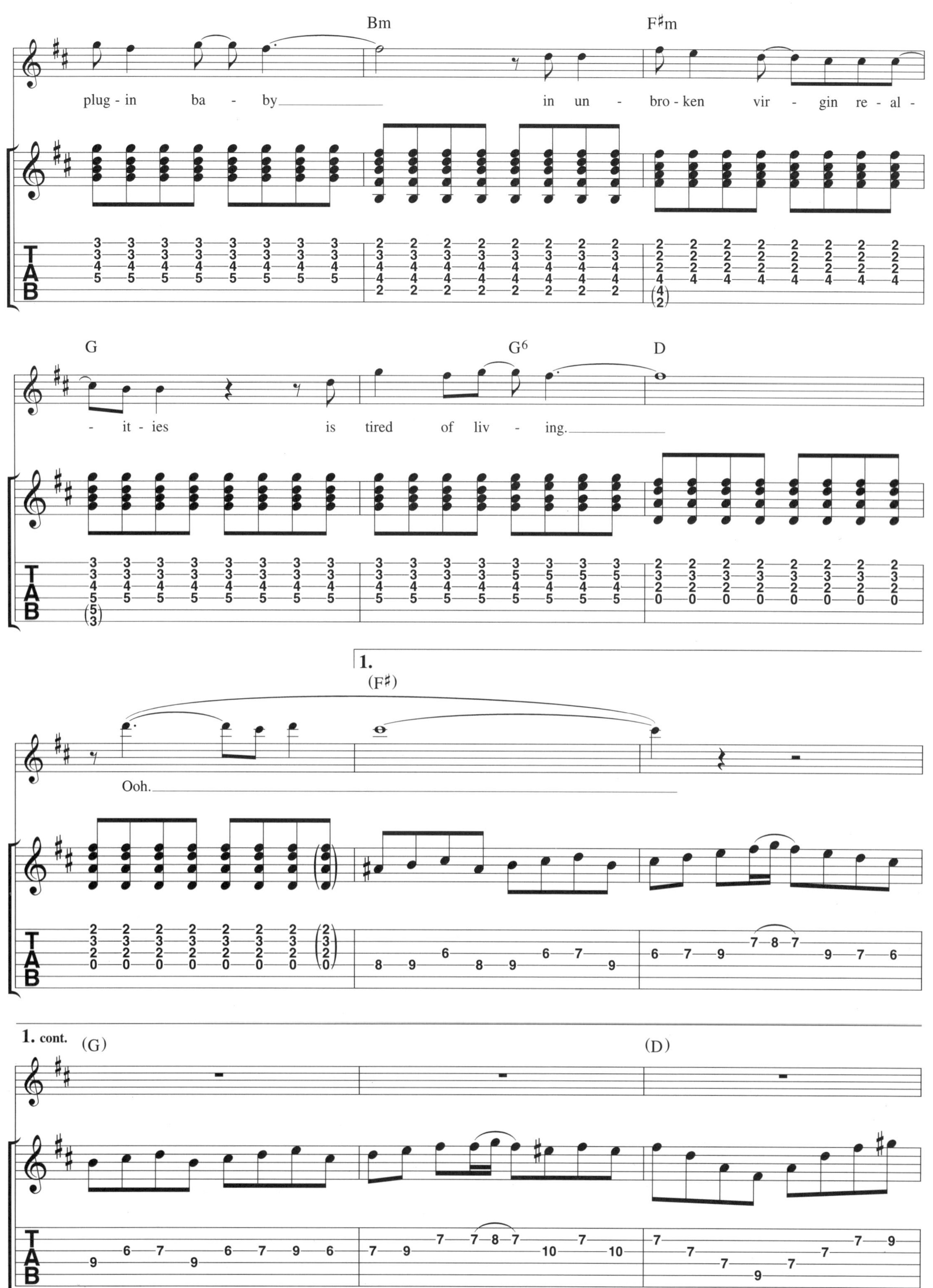

Bm
F#m
plug - in ba - by______________ in un - bro - ken vir - gin re - al -
G
G6
D
- it - ies is tired of liv - ing.______________
1.
(F#)
Ooh.
1. cont. (G)
(D)

1. cont.
(F#)
B
1/2
2.
(F#)
And I've seen your lov - - ing,
(G)
(D)
mine is gone,
B
1/2
(F#)
and I've been in trou - ble
(G)

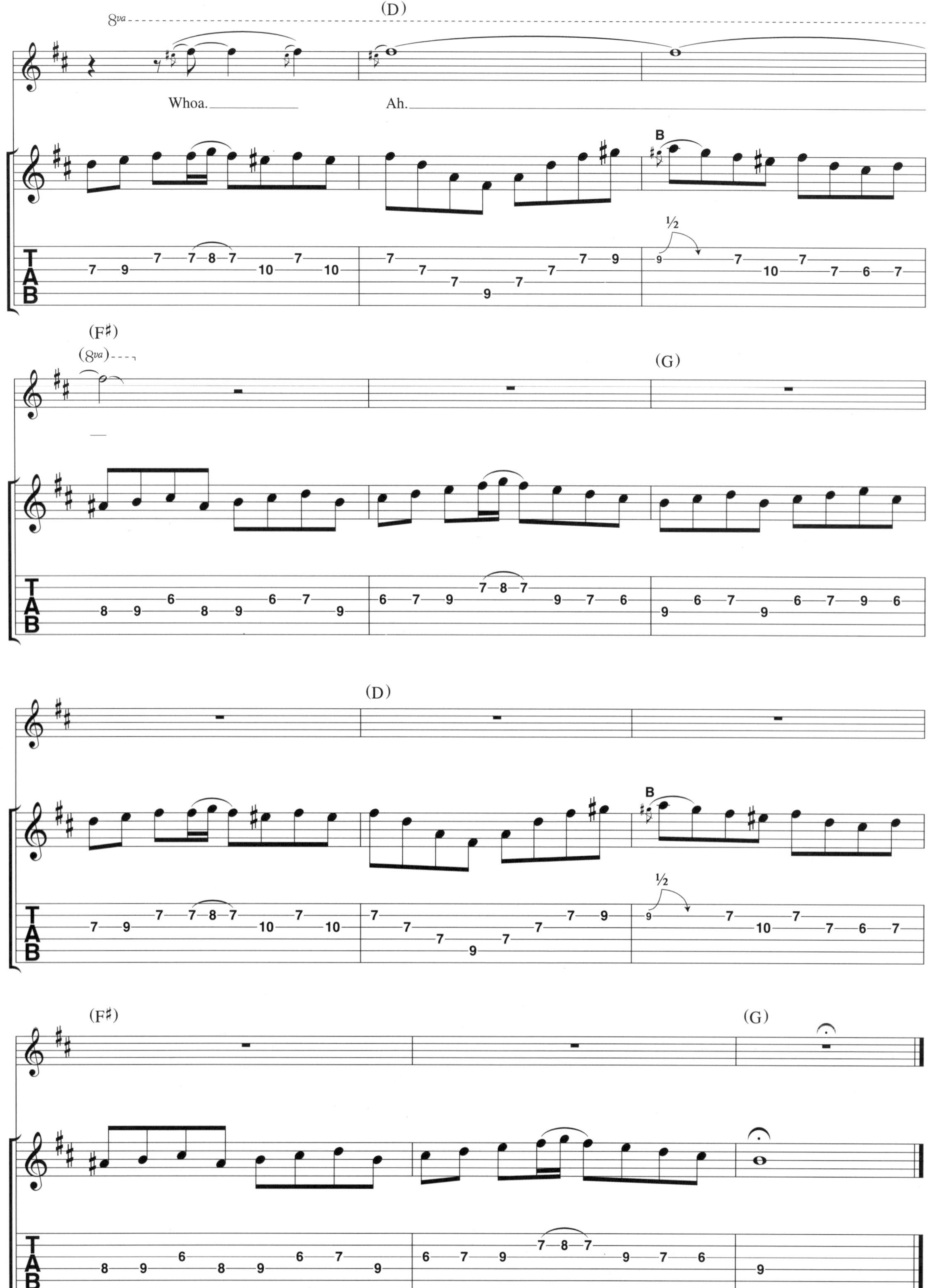

(D)
Whoa.
Ah.
(F♯)
(G)
(D)
(F♯)
(G)
23

just a day

Words & Music by Grant Nicholas

Intro

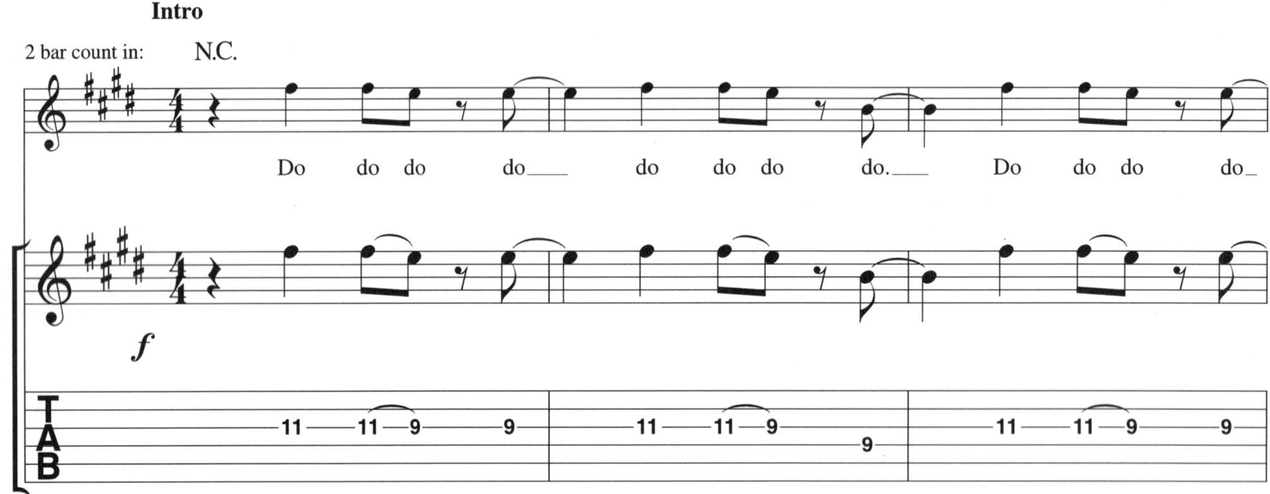

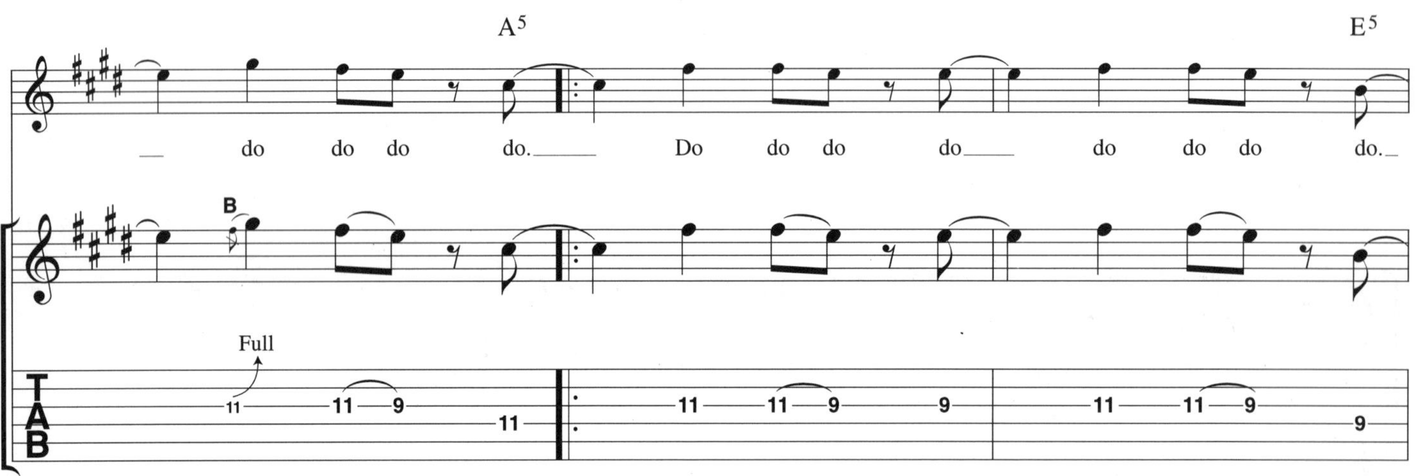

Verse

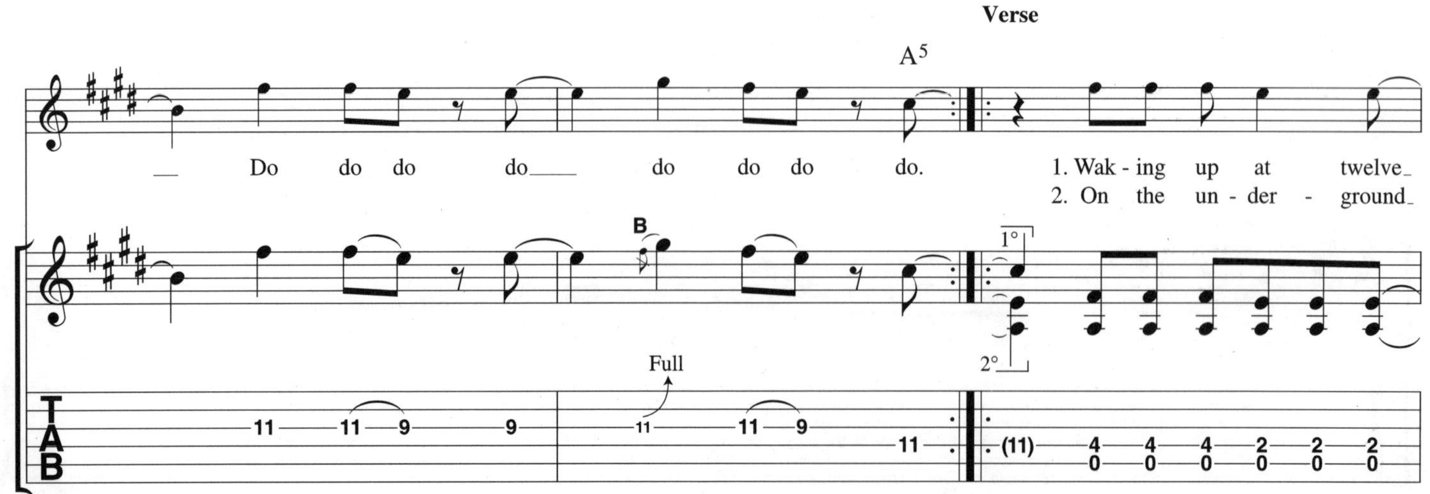

in my clothes a - gain,____ feel-ing head ex - plode____ from a night of gin.____
with the freaks__ and frowns____ look-in' at the world____ through sil - ver clouds.____
An - oth - er night out____ late.
But they all come____ down.
I don't wan - na drink,____ don't wan - na be a clown,
I got - ta rise a - bove____ the e - mo - tion - al flame,
got - ta get my feet____ back on the ground,____
got - ta cut these ropes____ a - round my hands,____

E5
C#m
be - fore it pulls me in.
pull my - self around.
E5
How come it end - ed up like this?
C#m
G#m
And who's gon - na catch me when I'm
Chorus
A
Aadd9
E
Badd11
C#m
go - in' down to hit the ground a - gain? All

Aadd9
C#m7
by my - self _____ (Wak-ing up at three in my clothes a - gain.)
Esus2
Badd11
'Cause I don't wan - na drag you down, _____ hold you down, _____
Aadd9
E
Badd11
_____ 'cause you're a friend. I blame my -
Aadd9
C#m7
F#7sus4
- self. (Feel my head ex - plode from a night of gin.) I guess you think it's

1.
A5
fun - ny now,___ fun - ny now.___
1. cont.
E5
A5
Do do do do___ do do do do.___ Do do do do___ do do do do.___
B
Full
1. cont.
E5
A5
___ Do do do do___ do do do do.___ Do do do do___ do.
B
Full
2.
A5
fun - ny now,___ fun - ny now.___

B5 C#5 G#5 A5
N.C. C#5 B5 G#5 A5
1. N.C.
2. A5 G#5 F#5
Chorus
(E)
(B add 11)
(A add 9)
All by my - self
(C#m7)
(E sus2)
'cause I don't wan - na drag you down,
mp

(Badd11)
(Aadd9)
(E)
drag you down,________________ 'cause you're a friend. I
(Badd11)
(Aadd9)
blame my - self.
(C#m7)
(F#7sus4)
(A5)
I guess you think it's fun - ny now,___ fun - ny now._______________
It's such a shame. All by my -
E
Badd11
f

Aadd9
C#m7
- self
'cause I don't wan - na
Esus2
Badd11
Aadd9
drag you down,___
drag you down,___
'cause you're a
E
Badd11
Aadd9
friend. I blame my - self.
1.
C#m7
F#7sus4
A5
I guess you think it's fun - ny now,___ fun -

1. cont.
2.
A5
- ny now. It's such a shame. fun - ny now, fun -
- ny now.
Do do do do. Do do do do.
Do do do do. Do do do do. Do do do do.
Do do do do. Do do do do.
TAB
32

side

Words & Music by Fran Healy

Intro

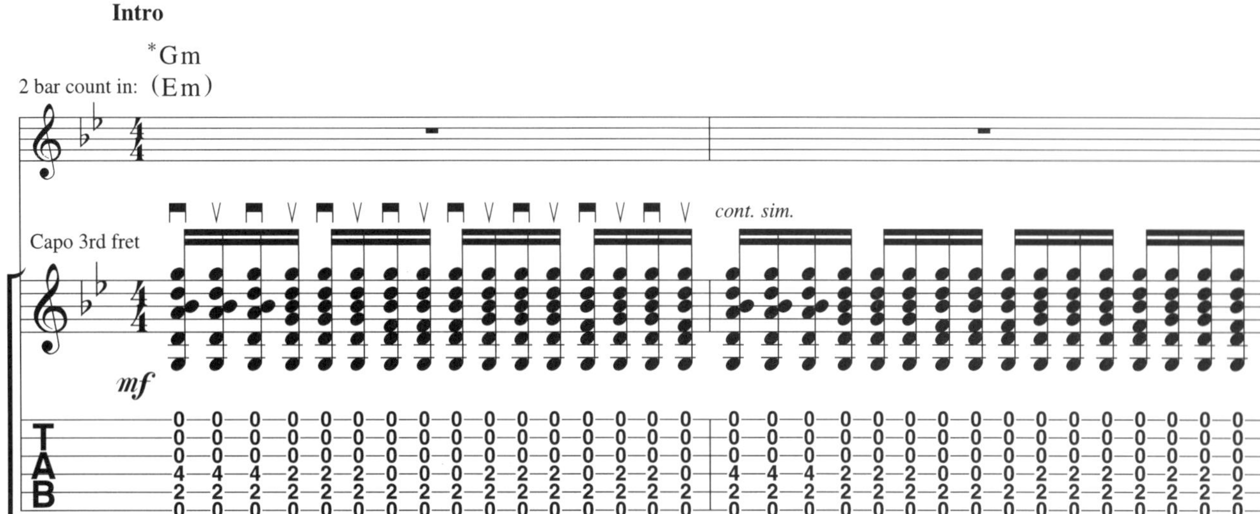

* Symbols in parentheses represent chord names with respect to capoed gtr. (Tab 0 = 3rd fret)
Symbols above represent actual sounding chords.

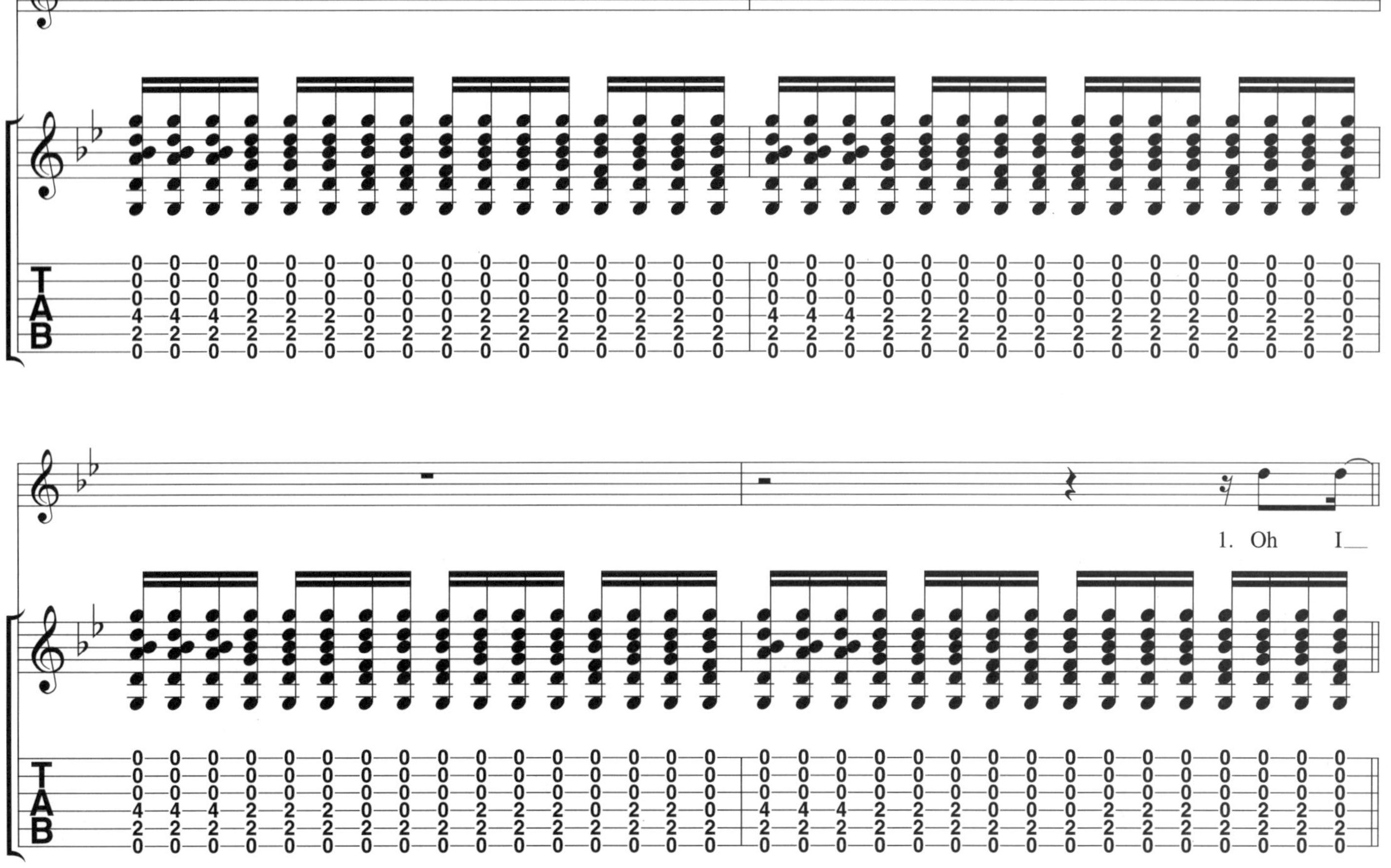

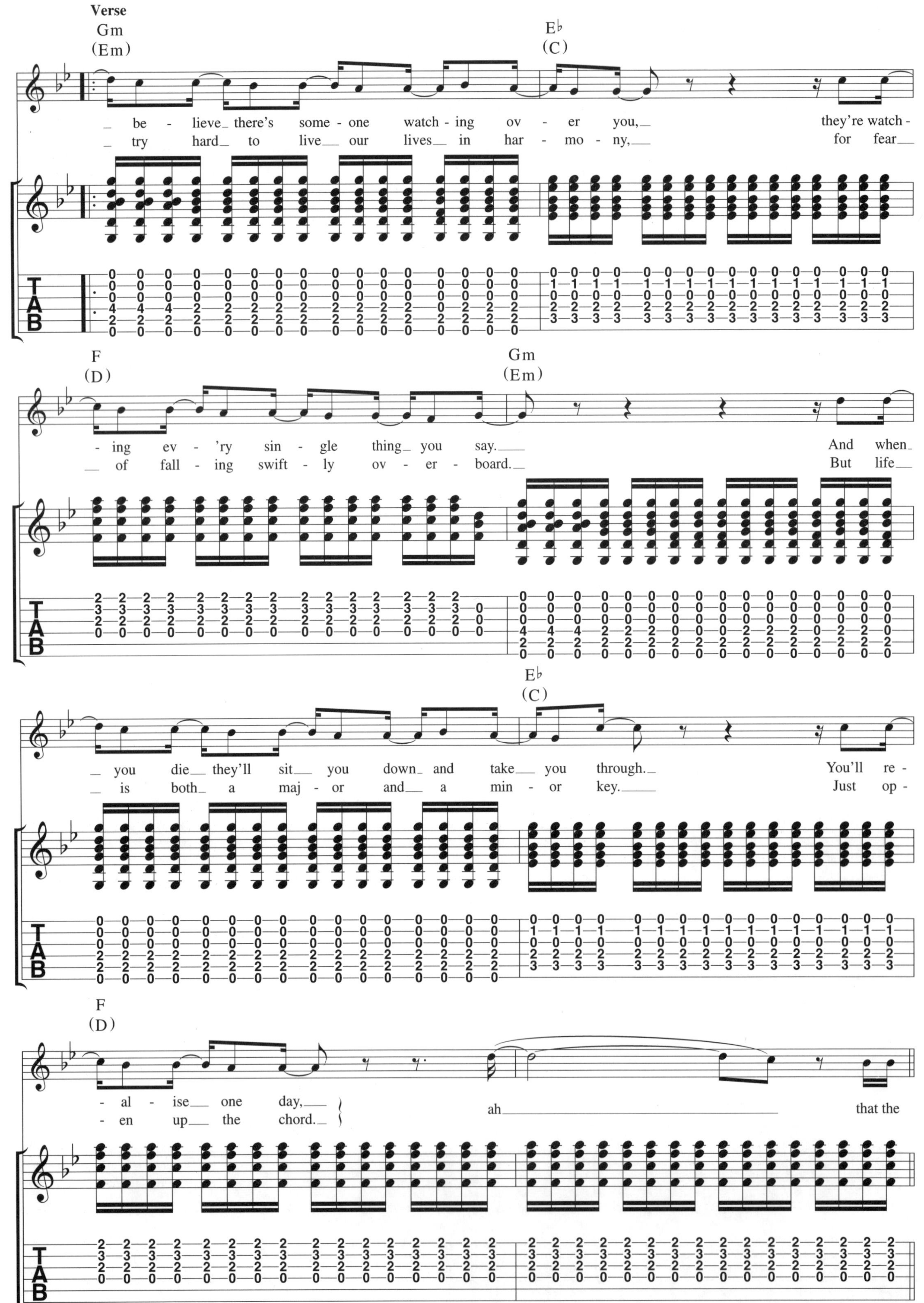

Verse
Gm
(Em)
Eb
(C)
be - lieve there's some - one watch - ing ov - er you, they're watch -
try hard to live our lives in har - mo - ny, for fear
F
(D)
Gm
(Em)
- ing ev - 'ry sin - gle thing you say. And when
of fall - ing swift - ly ov - er - board. But life
Eb
(C)
you die they'll sit you down and take you through. You'll re -
is both a maj - or and a min - or key. Just op -
F
(D)
- al - ise one day, ah that the
- en up the chord.
TAB

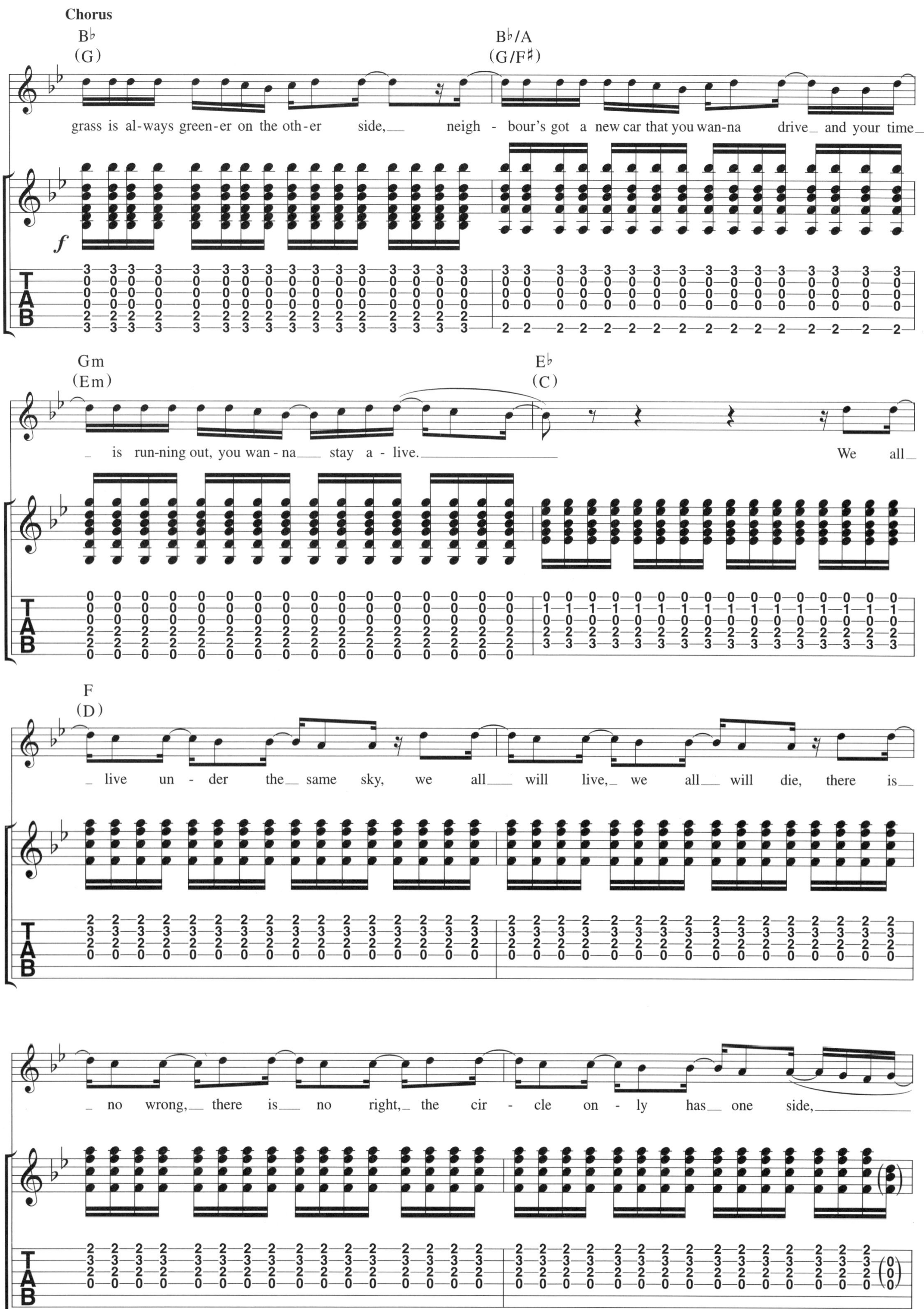

Chorus
Bb
(G)
Bb/A
(G/F#)
grass is al-ways green-er on the oth-er side,__ neigh - bour's got a new car that you wan-na drive_ and your time_
f
Gm
(Em)
Eb
(C)
_ is run-ning out, you wan - na__ stay a - live.__ We all_
F
(D)
_ live un - der the_ same sky, we all__ will live,_ we all__ will die, there is_
_ no wrong,__ there is_ no right,_ the cir - cle on - ly has_ one side,__

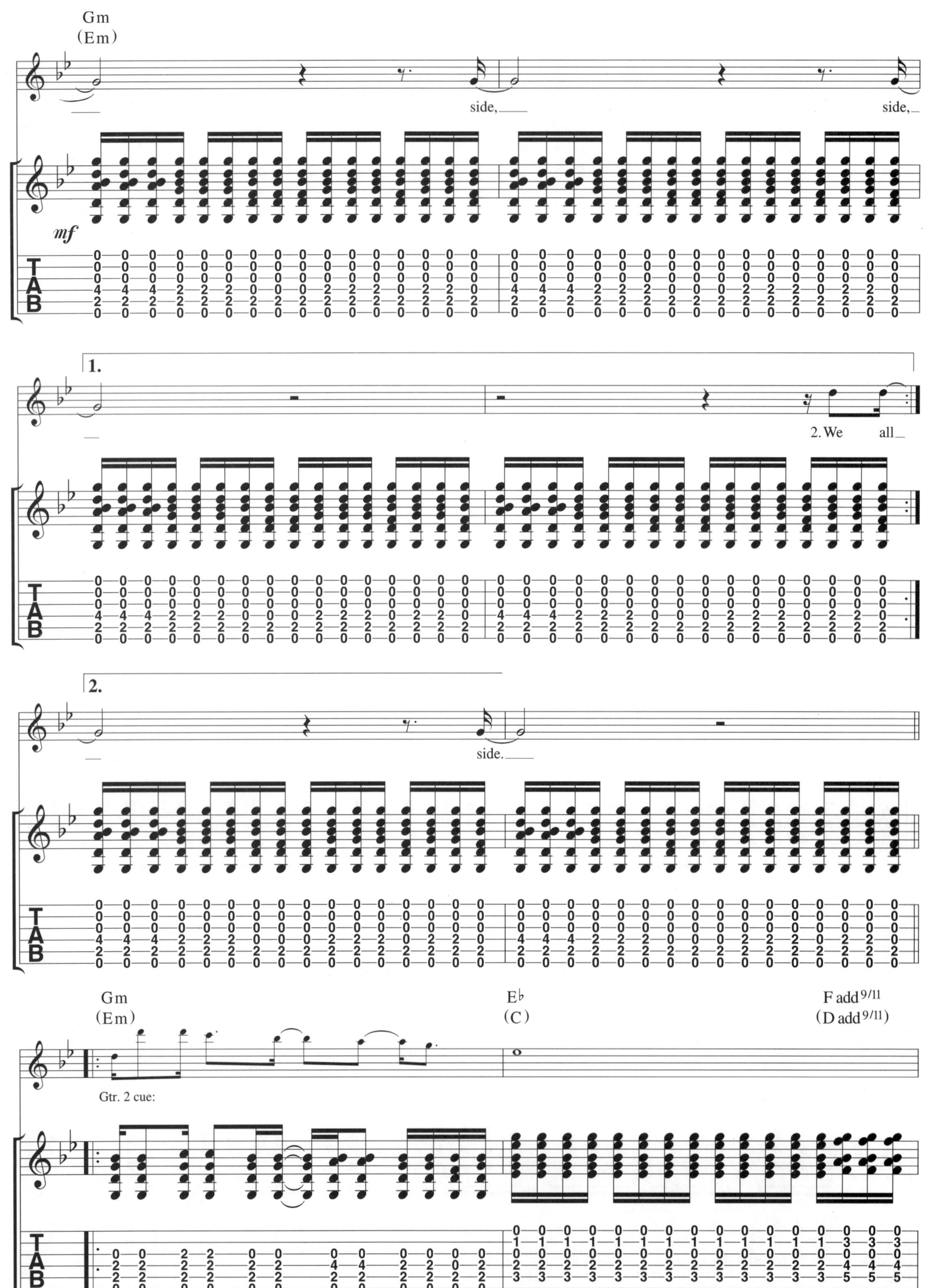

Gm
(Em)
mf
side,
side,
1.
2. We all
2.
side.
Gm
(Em)
Eb
(C)
F add 9/11
(D add 9/11)
Gtr. 2 cue:
TAB

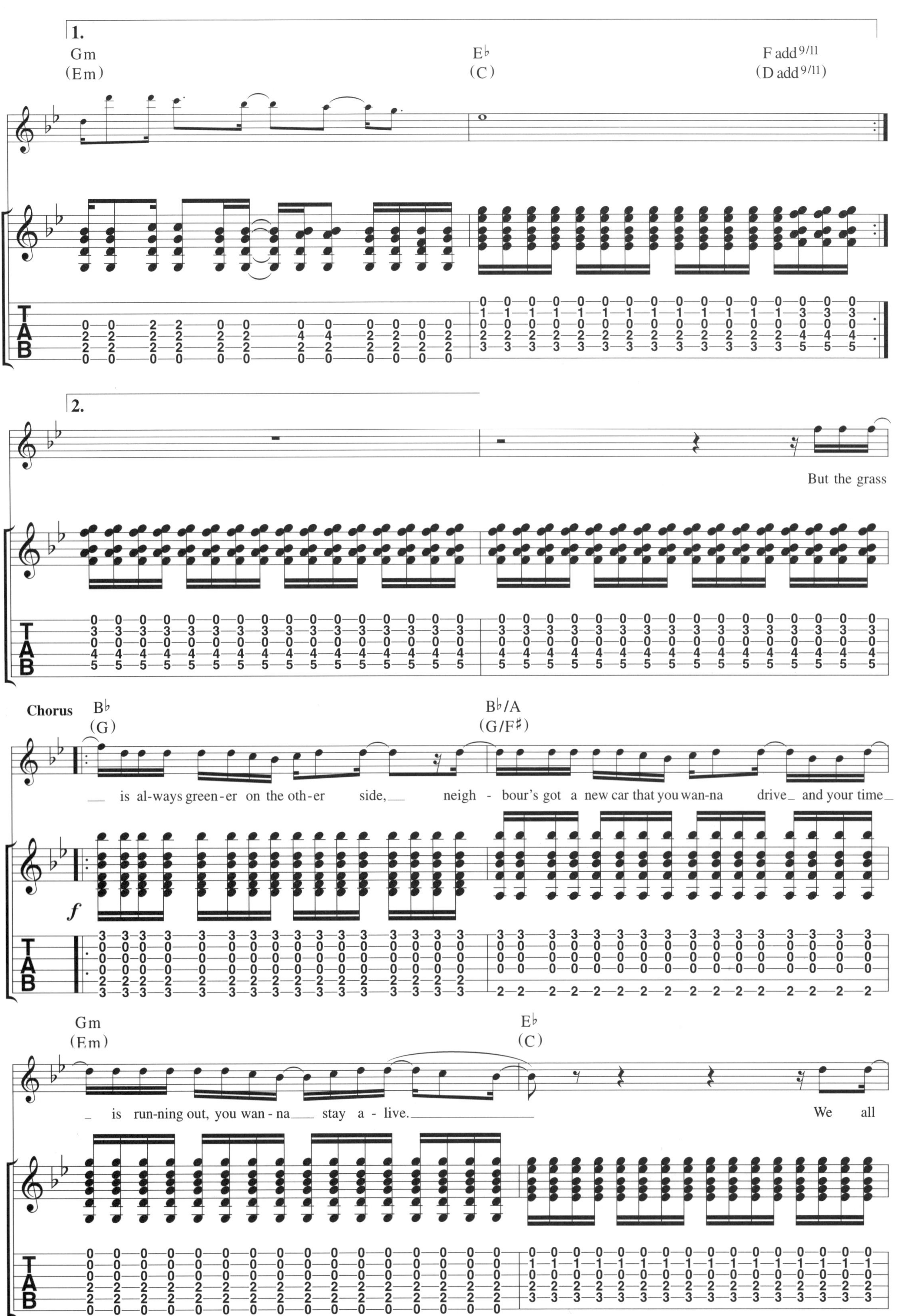

1.
Gm
(Em)
E♭
(C)
F add 9/11
(D add 9/11)
T A B
2.
But the grass
T A B
Chorus
B♭
(G)
B♭/A
(G/F♯)
f
__ is al-ways green-er on the oth-er side,__ neigh-bour's got a new car that you wan-na drive__ and your time__
T A B
Gm
(Em)
E♭
(C)
__ is run-ning out, you wan-na__ stay a-live.__ We all
T A B

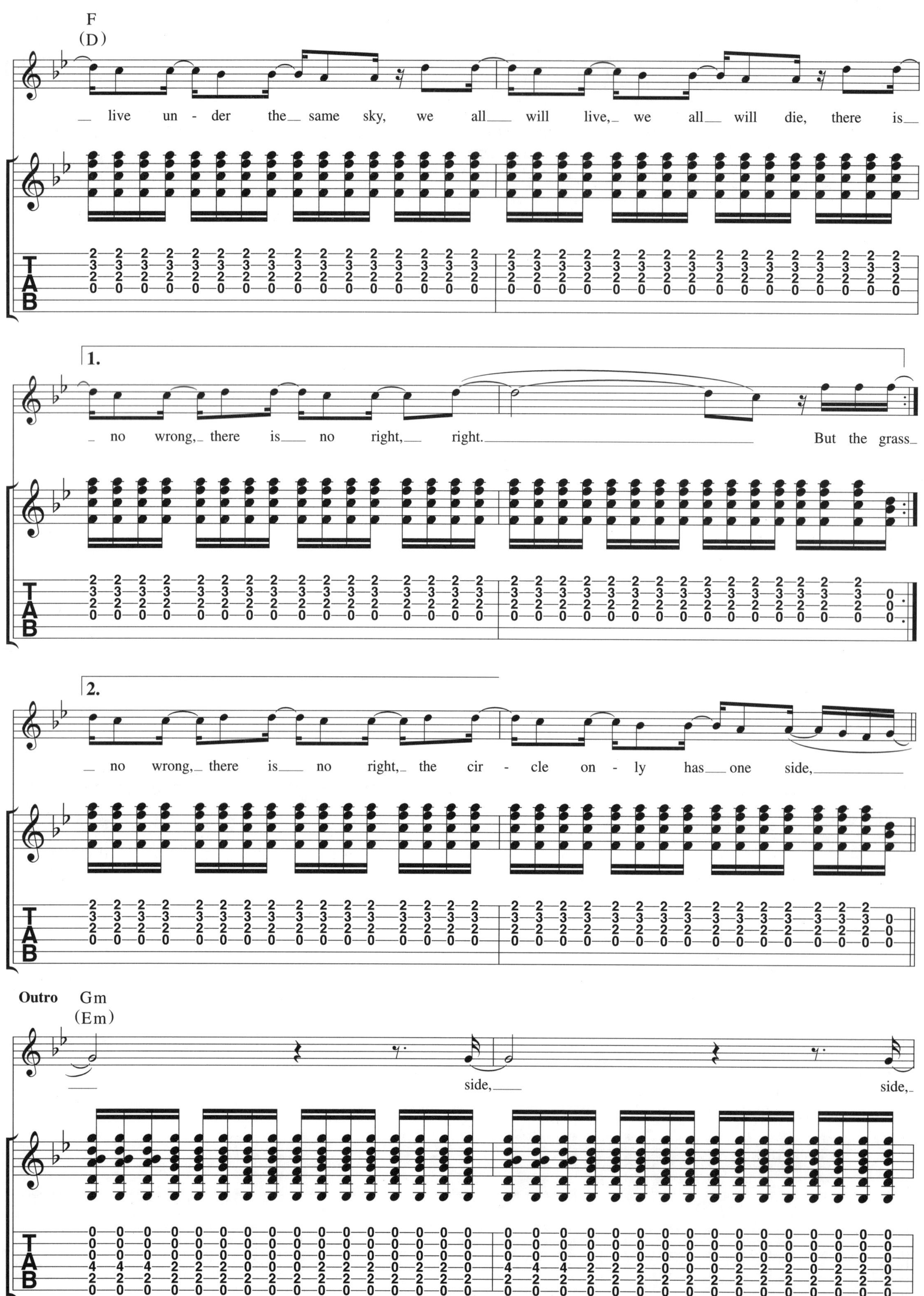

F
(D)
_ live un-der the_ same sky, we all_ will live,_ we all will die, there is_
1.
_ no wrong,_ there is_ no right,_ right._ But the grass_
2.
_ no wrong,_ there is_ no right,_ the cir-cle on-ly has_ one side,_
Outro   Gm
(Em)
_ side,_ side,_

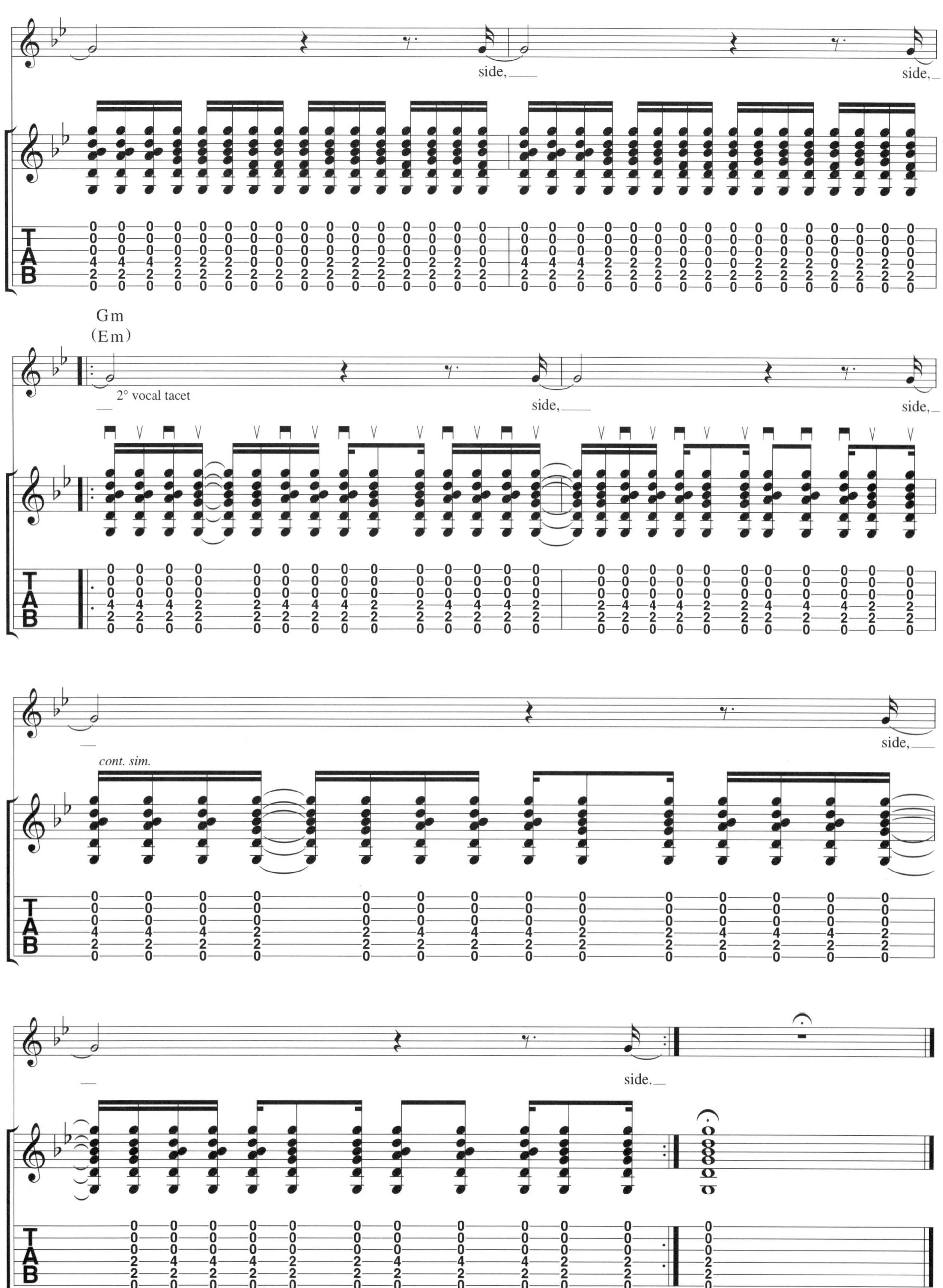

side,
Gm
(Em)
2° vocal tacet
side,
side,
side,
cont. sim.
side.

sunrise

Words & Music by Jarvis Cocker, Nick Banks, Candida Doyle, Stephen Mackey & Mark Webber

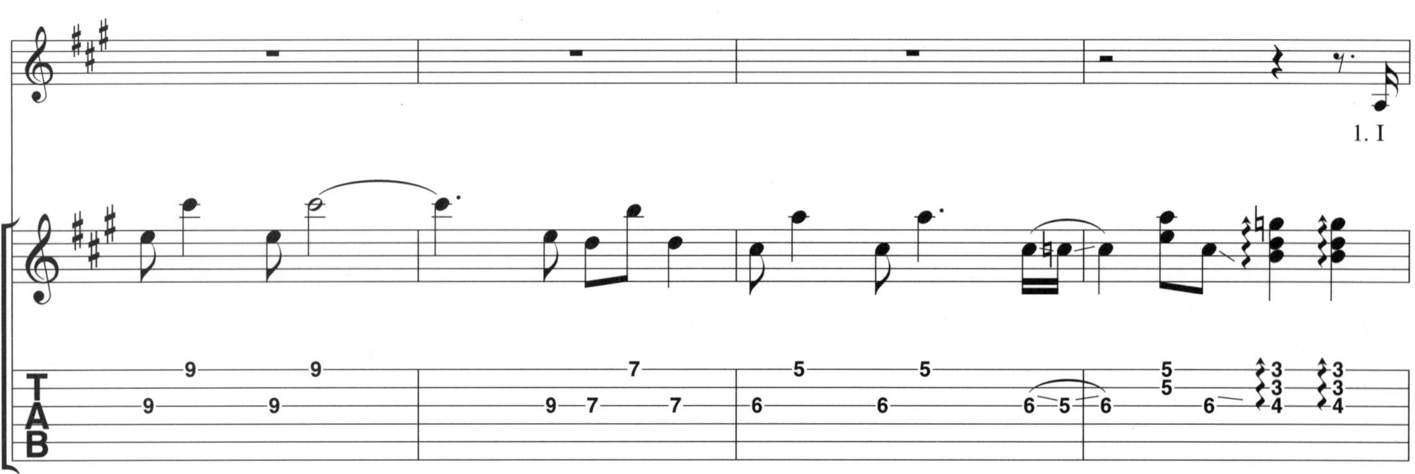

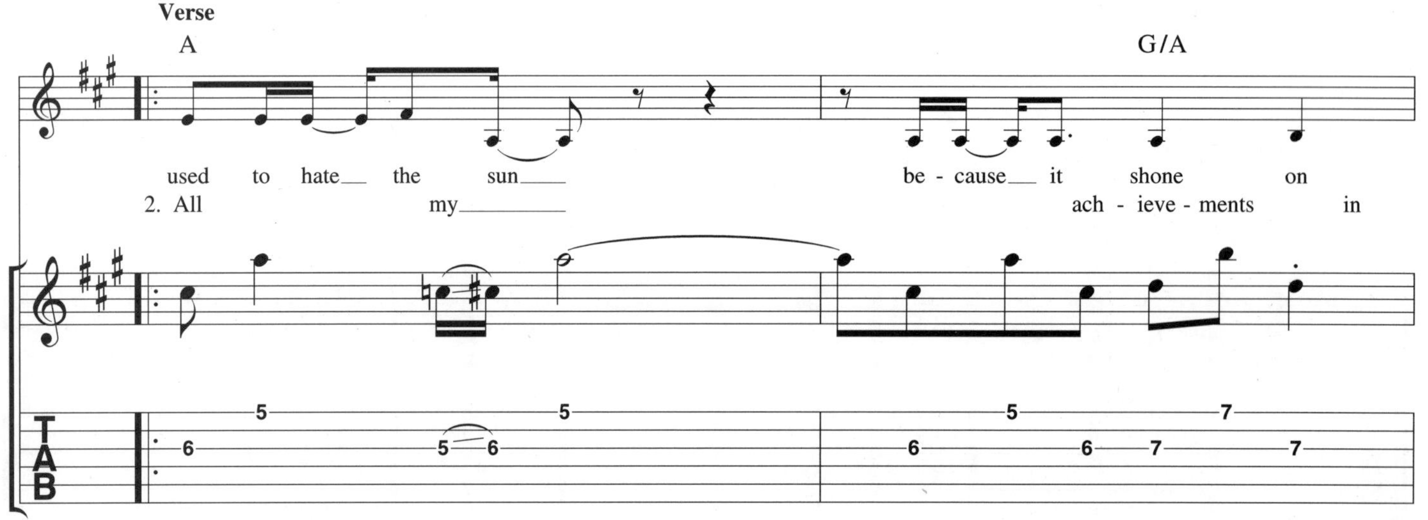

A
D/A
ev - 'ry - thing I've done, made me feel that
days of yore range from path-etic
A
G/A
all that I had done was ov - er - fill the ash-tray of
to piss poor but all that's gonna
1. A
my life.
2. A
change.
Be-cause
Chorus
G
A
here comes sun - rise.
41

G
Yeah, it's your
A
sun - rise.
I used to hide from the sun,
mp
G7/A
A
cont. sim.
tried to live my whole life un - der - ground.
Mm,
D/A
A
why d'ya have to rise and ru - in all my fun? Just turn ov -
slowly cresc.

G/A   A
- er close the cur - tains on the day. But
Chorus
G   A
here comes sun - rise.
mf
G
Yeah, it's your
A   D
sun - rise. When you've been a - wake all night

A   Dm   A
long   and you feel like crash-ing___ out at dawn.   But you've

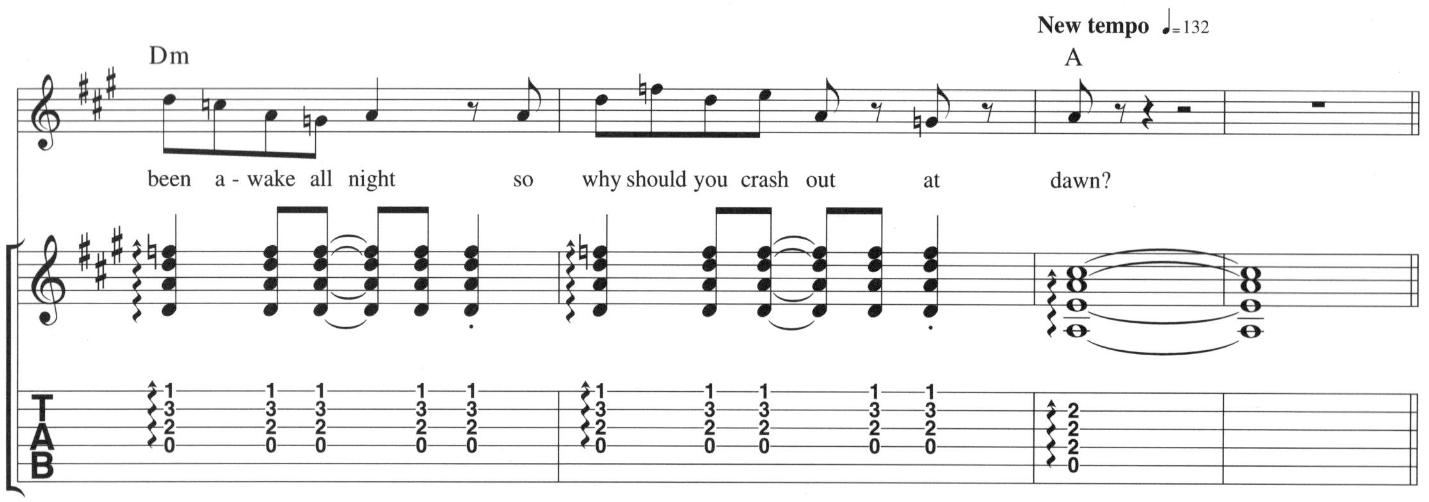

New tempo ♩=132
Dm   A
been a-wake all night   so   why should you crash out   at   dawn?

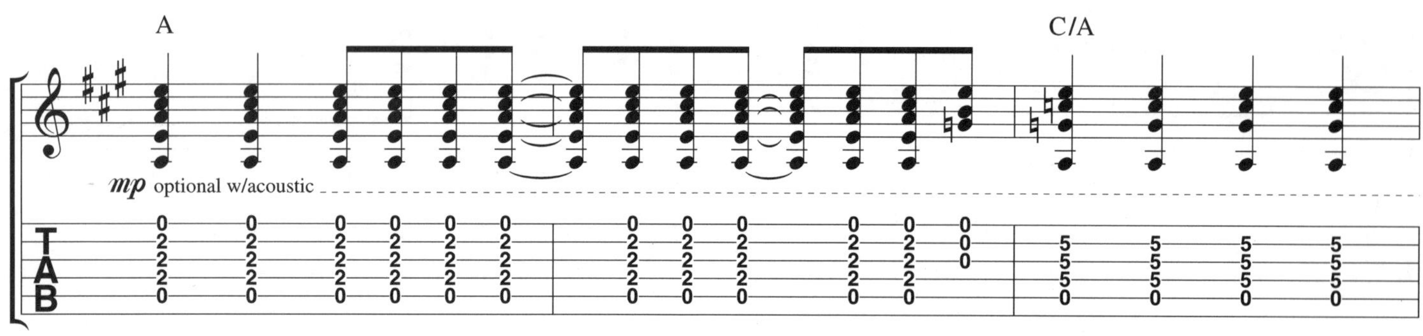

A   C/A
mp optional w/acoustic

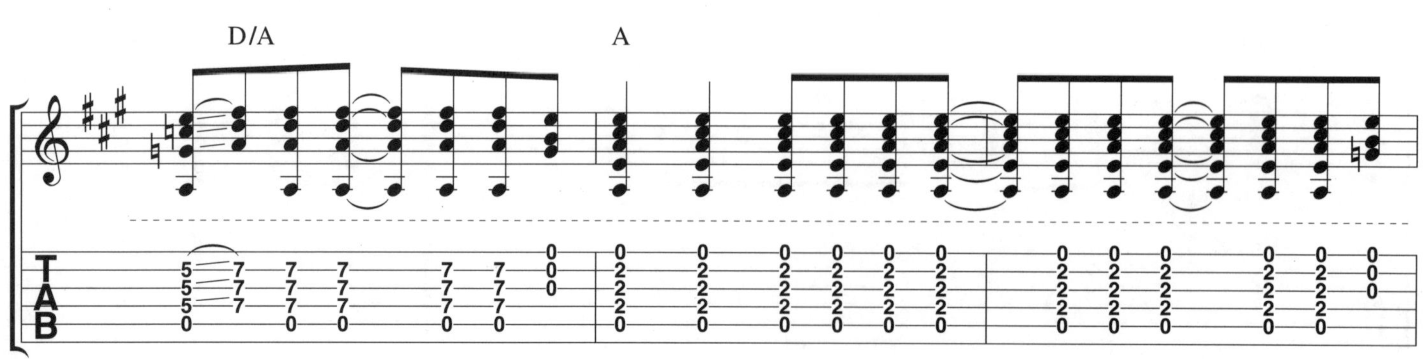

D/A   A

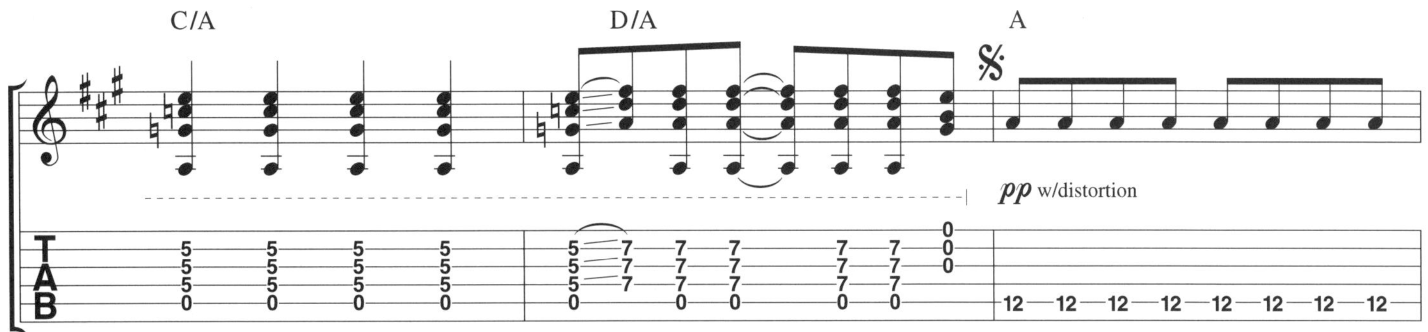

C/A
D/A
A
pp w/distortion

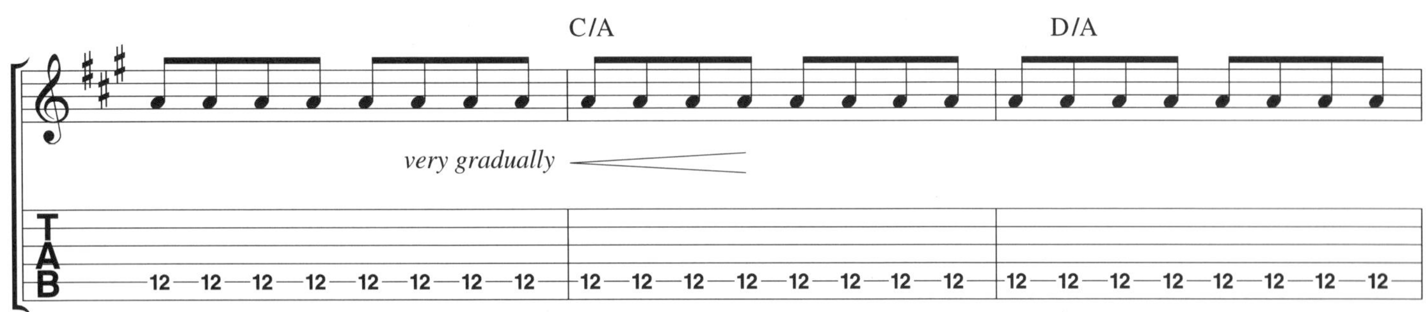

C/A
D/A
very gradually

A
C/A
mp

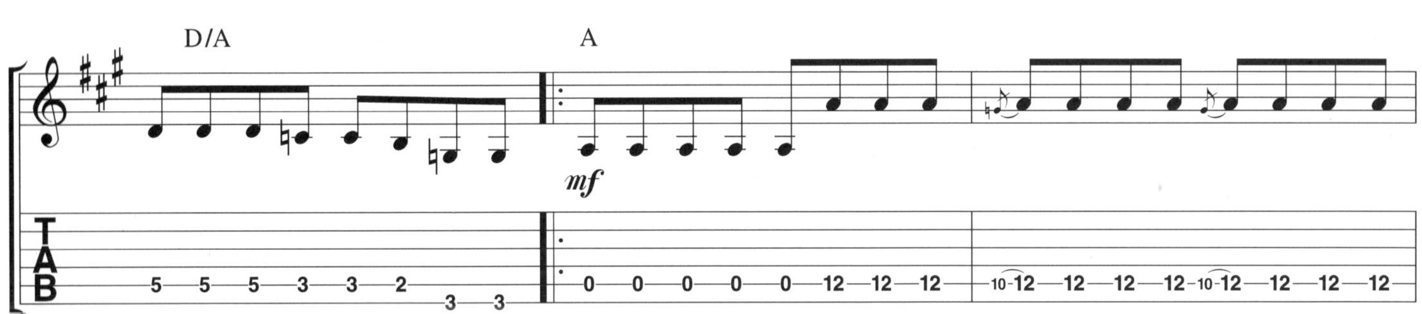

D/A
A
mf

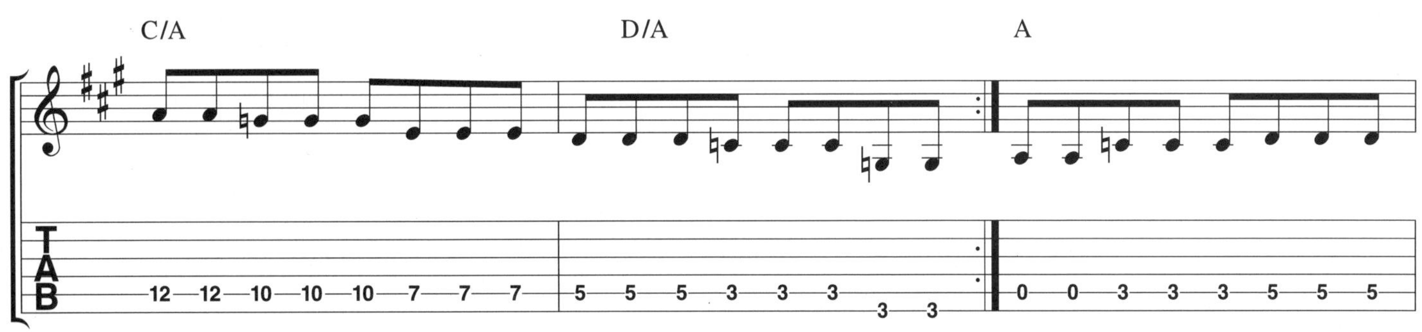

C/A
D/A
A

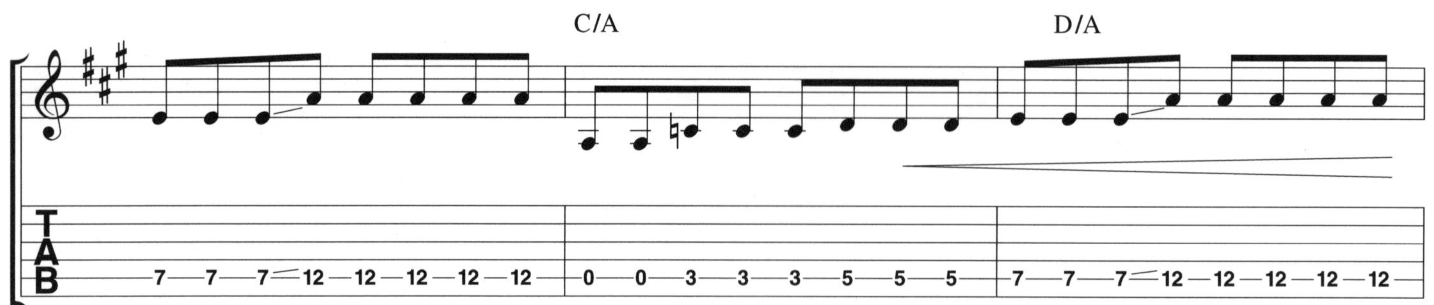

C/A
D/A

A
C/A

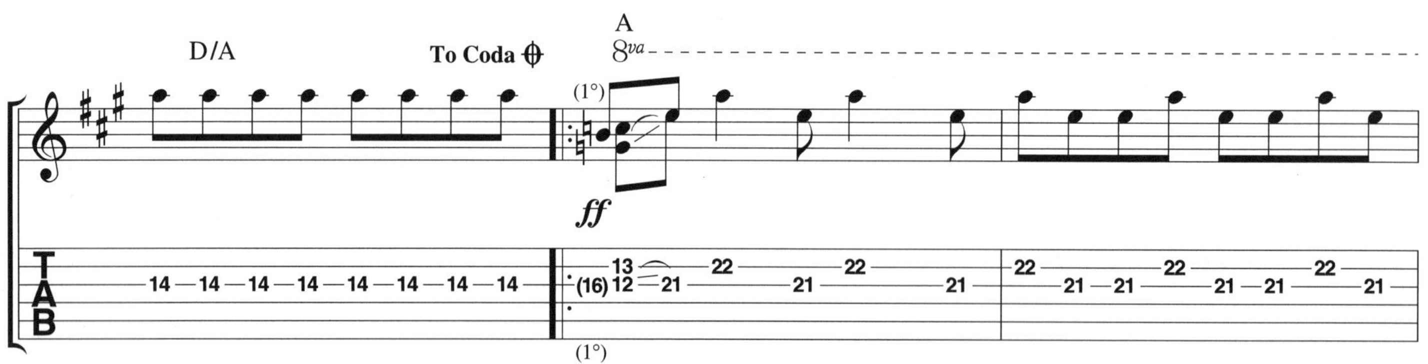

D/A
To Coda
A
8va
(1°)
ff
(1°)

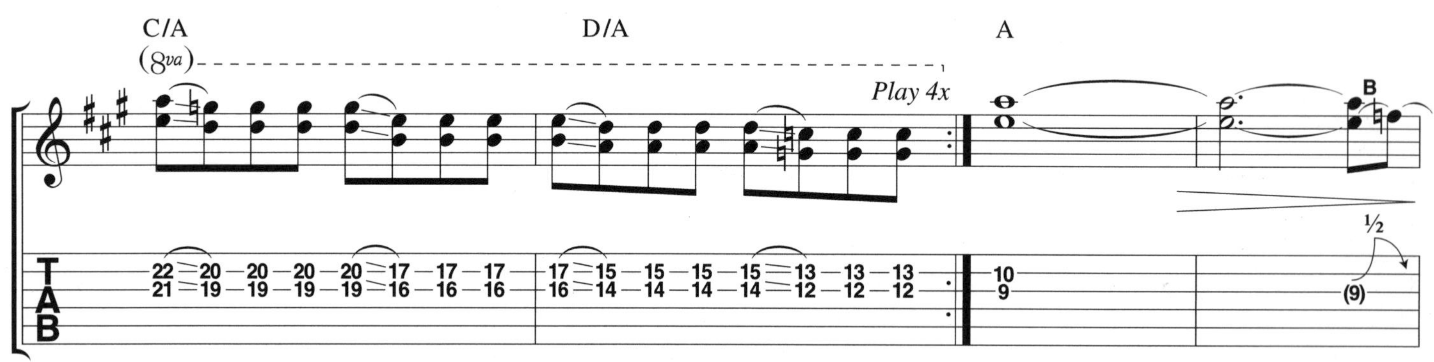

C/A
D/A
A
(8va)
Play 4x
B
½

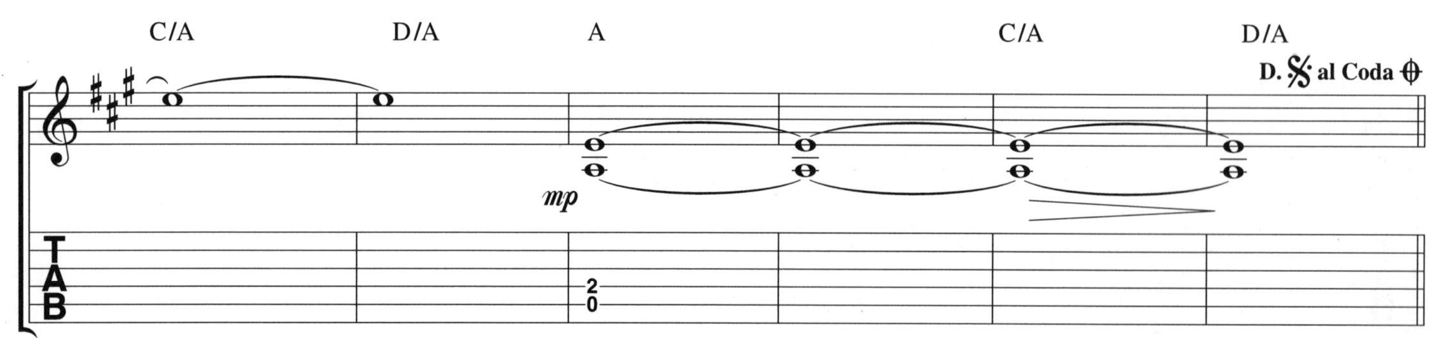

C/A
D/A
A
C/A
D/A
D. S. al Coda
mp

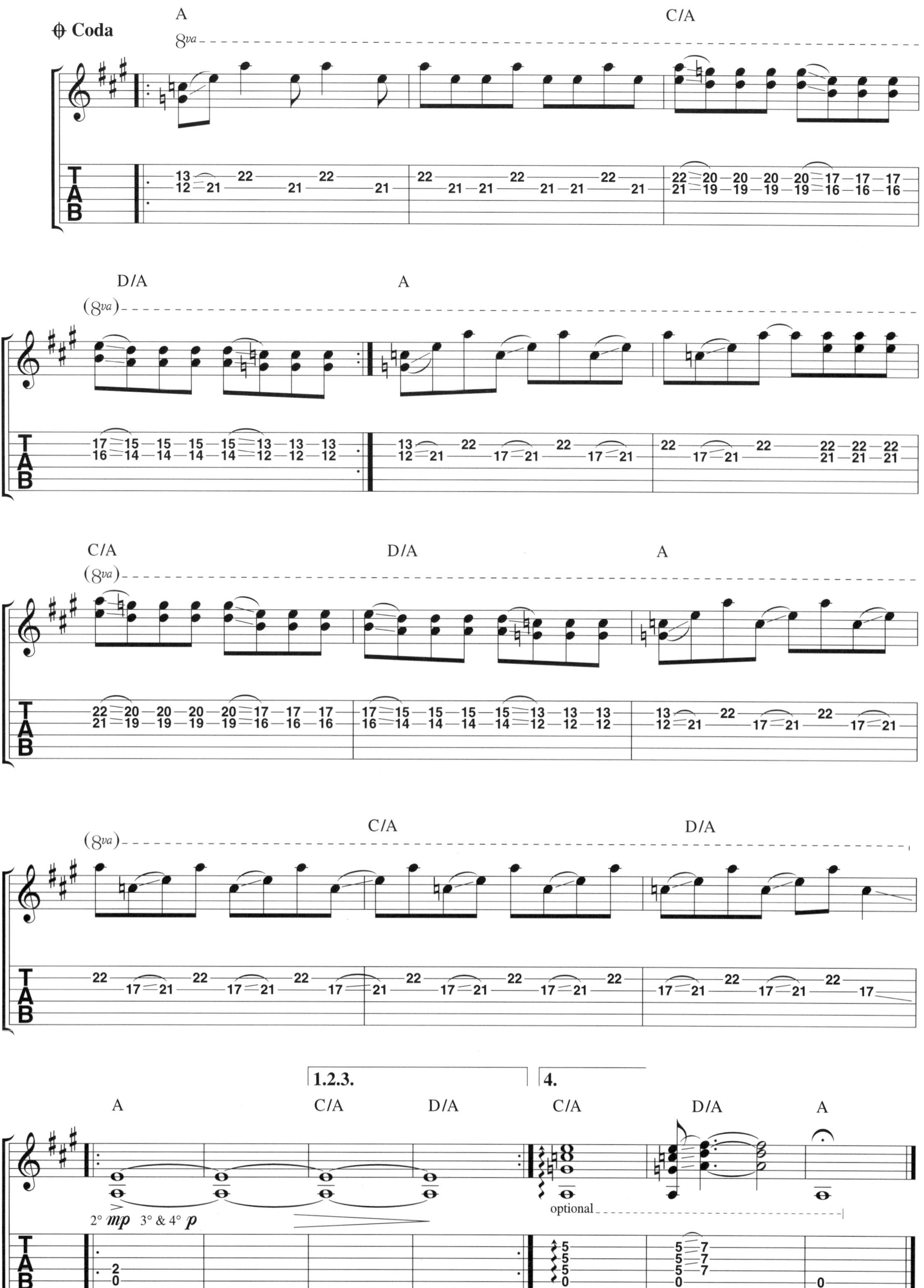
Coda
A
C/A
8va
D/A
A
C/A
D/A
A
C/A
D/A
1.2.3.
4.
A
C/A
D/A
C/A
D/A
A
optional
2° mp 3° & 4° p

Exclusive distributors:
Music Sales Limited
8-9 Frith Street,
London W1D 3JB, England.
Music Sales Pty Limited
120 Rothschild Avenue,
Rosebery, NSW 2018, Australia.

Order No. AM973907
ISBN 0-7119-9345-9
This book © Copyright 2002
by Wise Publications

Music compiled and arranged by Arthur Dick
Music processed by Andrew Shiels
Cover photograph courtesy of London Features International
Printed in the United Kingdom by
Printwise (Haverhill) Limited, Suffolk.

CD recorded, mixed and mastered by Jonas Persson
All guitars by Arthur Dick
Bass by Paul Townsend
Drums by Brett Morgan

Your Guarantee of Quality